THE GOLDEN BOOK OF
CRACOW

Text by
GRZEGORZ RUDZIŃSKI

Photographs by
ANDREA PISTOLESI

BONECHI

Dystrybutor w Polsce:
"GALAKTYKA" sp. z o. o. Łódź
Fax. 42 791335 Tel. 42 406509

ISBN 83-86447-46-X

CRACOW

Publication created and designed by Casa Editrice Bonechi
Project and graphic realization: Sonia Gottardo
Picture research: Monica Bonechi
Videolayout: "m&m", Florence
Editing: Simonetta Giorgi

Text: Grzegorz Rudziński

Translation: Heather MacKay Roberts.

© Copyright 1996 by
CASA EDITRICE BONECHI
Via Cairoli 18/b - Tel. +39 55 576841 - Fax +39 55 5000766
50131 Florence - Italy
e-mail:bonechi@bonechi.it
Internet:www.bonechi.it

Printed in Italy by the
Centro Stampa Editoriale Bonechi.

Photographs from the Archives of
Casa Editrice Bonechi taken by
Andrea Pistolesi.

Illustrations on pages 3, 5, plan on page 86 and map of Cracow:
a courtesy of Galaktyka sp. zo.o. Łódź

ISBN 88-8029-614-0

* * *

One of the illustrations from the *Chronicles* of H. Schedel, published in Nuremberg in 1493: a view of Cracow in the late fifteenth century. The Wawel is on the hill overlooking the city. On the far side of a branch of the Vistula, which later dried up, and within the city walls stands Kazimierz - today one of the suburbs of Cracow.

INTRODUCTION

"Cracow was not built in a day". The old Polish proverb underlines one of the essential features of this city, its extremely long history, extending back over thousands rather than hundreds of years. The period of prehistoric colonisation on the Jurassic hills along the banks of the Vistula was much longer than the thousand years of the city's recorded history. Temporary settlements by nomads in the Palaeolithic period were followed by permanent ones some five thousand years ago. Remains of the earliest settlements have been found on the Wawel hill, which was to become the political centre of the community. Archaeological excavations bear witness to the uninterrupted local production of objects, from the tools of the Neolithic period to later pieces in bronze and iron. The mining of metals began in the area in about 1700 B.C. Cracow and the surrounding territory came

under the influence of Lusazian, Pomeranian and more recently Przeworsk culture. Numerous objects from the Roman period (1st-4th centuries A.D.) reflect the lively commercial relationship between Cracow and the Empire. The oldest monument in Cracow dates to the 7th century and is a mound some 16 metres high known as the Krak tumulus. We can trace the beginnings of the Vislani state, to the 8th century when a small fortified city (gród), with surrounding towns (podgrodzie), was built on the Wawel hill, probably the seat of the capital of the Vislani. In the course of the 9th and 10th centuries Cracow came under the influence first of Greater Moravia and then of Bohemia. It is to this period that we date the earliest document relating to Cracow, in which the name of the city, transcribed in Arabic by a certain Ibrahim Ibn-Yaqub (a Jewish merchant from Spain), can be interpreted as

3

Karaka or Krakua. In the same year 965 the marriage was celebrated between the Bohemian princess Dobrava and Duke Mieszko, leader of the Polani and resident in Gniezno, capital of Great Poland. This union determined Cracow's future relations with Poland. It was not long before Mieszko made war against his Bohemian brother-in-law and took possession of the "State of Cracow" which he left to his son, Bolesław, called the Intrepid. After the death of his father, Bolesław, who had already established Cracow as his permanent seat, united all the Polish territories to the north to his kingdom, and so became the first Polish monarch over what came to be known as Little Poland. In 1000 Cracow became an episcopal see and therefore gained importance over other Polish cities. It was in Cracow rather than in Gniezno in 1076 that Duke Bolesław the Bold was consecrated King of Poland, and his successor Władysław Herman minted coins bearing the name of Cracow. Bolesław the wry-mouthed, son of Władysław, divided the kingdom into duchies to be ruled over by his sons, with Cracow left to the eldest. What sort of city was Cracow at that time? The romanesque cathedral, the stone castle, seat of the royal family, and the wood and stone citadel surrounded by ramparts were all built on the hill of Wawel. To the north of the hill Okol continued to expand, a completely independent city with fortified walls, containing the romanesque churches dedicated to St Ignatius and St Andrew. The breakdown of the feudal system marked a period of continuous unrest but also of continuous progress in Cracow. While individual representatives of the various branches of the Pilast dynasty fought over the city, Germanic hordes began to penetrate vast areas of sparsely populated Polish territory. When in 1241 the Tartar armies invaded southern Poland, Cracow suffered serious damage. The accession to power in 1243 of Boleslaw the Chaste, who reigned in Little Poland for some twenty-six years, marked the beginning of a period of peace and development fostered by his enlightened policies. On 6 June 1257 the Duke conferred the "privilege of location" on the city, bringing an end to the period of its early history. The 13th century witnessed the emergence of the gothic city with buildings built of brick in contrast to the earlier, mainly stone, romanesque architecture, and it is the city's gothic character which still prevails today. In 1287 when the Cracow was threatened by renewed attacks from invading Tartar armies the strong city walls then protected it from destruction by the barbarians. Between the 13th and 14th centuries the city was the scene of the struggle for the restoration of the Polish monarchy; there had been no king since the abdication of Bolesław the Bold in 1079 as no member of the Piast dynasty had been able to recover the crown. Although Przemysł II had himself consecrated King of Poland in 1295 it was not until the coronation of Władysław the Short, who took con-trol of Cracow in 1306, that the monarchy became securely reinvested in the Piast dynasty. In 1312 Władysław overcame the opposition of the city's hostile German-speaking mercantile patrician class and in 1320 was crowned in Wawel Cathedral where he was to be buried in 1333. He was the first of the Polish kings to be buried there and the building became the royal burial place. The accession to the throne of Casimir the Great (1333-70) marks the beginning of Cracow's ascendancy which lasted some 230 years. Casimir the Great founded the University in 1364, and built a fortified city on the other side of the Vistula, Kazimierz, which eventually became absorbed by Cracow. He enlarged the textile industry and encouraged local trade. His niece, Jadwiga, left all her jewels to the University to finance its modernisation. Her marriage to the Lithuanian Grand-duke, Jagiellon, signalled the rise of a new dynasty in the Polish kingdom. The Jagiellonian period of Polish history coincided with her greatest military strength and economic prosperity. Her solid alliance with Lithuania ensured her unrivalled dominance over neighbouring states. In 1414 Jagiellon, together with his brother Vitoldo, did much to free Poland from the oppressive power of the Teutonic order. Under Casimir Jagiellon (1447-1492) Poland regained control over access to the Baltic and, as a result of a dispute with Moldavia, recovered the ports on the Black Sea. There was considerable commercial expansion in the Polish cities and Cracow was among those which increased in size and prosperity. In the second half of the 15th century the Academy at Cracow attracted students from all over central Europe, including Nicholas Copernicus from 1491 to 1495. By the early 16th century interest in the humanist movement and the Renaissance brought about what later became known as "the golden century of Polish culture". In 1525 in Rynek Główny, the Market Square, in Cracow Albrecht Hohenzollern, last Grand Master of the Teutonic Order and the first duke of Prussia, paid homage to King Sigismund I in recognition of his sovereignty. As a result of Sigismund's marriage to a Sforza from Milan, the royal castle on Wawel hill was rebuilt in the Italian renaissance style, one of the finest monuments in that style north of the Alps. Court life flourished and high offices could be obtained by men of various nationalities and social backgrounds: Poles, Germans, Jews, Italians, Hungarians. Cracow became the centre of a thriving printing business and was of vital importance in the growth of the Polish language.

This short-lived period of brilliance was followed by steady decline. During the reign of Sigismund III Vasa (1587-1632) the country was involved in wars to the north, and the capital was transferred from Cracow to Warsaw. Cracow retained much of its ancient prestige and the Cathedral remained the site of the coronation of the Polish kings but during the two wars with

Sweden (1655-60 and 1703-21) the city suffered severe damage. At the beginning of the 18th century Poland became prey to the political ambitions of neighbouring states. After the second Partition, Tadeusz Kościuszko determined to safeguard what remained of Polish sovereignty, and on 24 March 1794 in Cracow proclaimed a national insurrection and declared himself leader of a revolutionary government. During one of his last campaigns when the revolutionary cause was virtually lost the Prussians sacked Cracow and carried off the royal treasure from the castle of Wawel. The city remained unscathed during the Napoleonic campaign, and the Congress of Vienna (1815) instituted the Republic of Cracow, a small state governed by the Poles. Throughout the 19th century the city played a leading role in Polish artistic and cultural life. The University slowly regained its prestige; Karol Olszewski and Zygmunt Wróblewski were of central importance in the Polish revival. In 1879 the National Museum was founded to house paintings and sculptures by Polish artists, including the monumental works of Jan Matejko, while the Czartoryski displays objects of national importance.

On 6 August 1914 the first troops under the command of Józef Piłsudski left Cracow to fight in defence of free Poland. During the period of Independent Poland Cracow became the fourth city after Warsaw, Łódź and Lvov. In the years of Nazi occupation during the second world war the Jewish population of Cracow was totally exterminated, a community which had enriched the history of the city for centuries. In the period after the war the main concern was for the reconstruction of the city and more recently for the preservation of her buildings threatened by acid rain from local industrial development. In 1978 Cracow was included on the UNESCO list of the twelve most remarkable architectural complexes in the world. The same year saw the election of the city's archbishop Karol Wojtyła as Pope John Paul II. The city is one of Poland's greatest tourist attractions and as an artistic and cultural centre equals Warsaw.

In recent years, as a result of the progressive expansion of gas heating and the control of harmful industries, the environment of Cracow has considerably improved. The successful protection and conservation of the city's historic monuments continues with the support of the Polish people.

A French print of the nineteenth century: the Barbican and the St Florian Gate, seen from the quarter of Kleparz.

Aerial view of Rynek Główny.

RYNEK GŁÓWNY (THE MARKET SQUARE)

The 13th-century quarter of the city has survived unaltered to the present day. Rynek Główny, one of the largest squares in medieval Europe, was laid down in 1257 as a slightly irregular square, some 200 metres on each side. The surrounding houses were built in the 14th and 15th centuries and have over the centuries been restored and in some instances rebuilt. The classical façades on a large number of the houses were built during restoration work from the 17th to the 19th centuries but many retain renaissance and baroque stone doorways, together with the original beams, porticoed courtyards and sections of the attic storeys. Among the most notable buildings on the square are the *Sukiennice*, the Town hall tower, the church dedicated to St Adalbert, the Zbaraskich Palace (at no. 20), the Palace of Ariete (at no.27), the especially fine Church of the Virgin Mary together with the monument to Adam Mickiewicz. The present level of the square is

some two metres higher than the original one, as we can see from the south side of the church of the Virgin Mary where the lower part of the wall has been revealed by archaeologists; note also the sunken level of the church of St Adalbert. A visit to Rynek Główny,not only gives us a chance to admire its architectural beauty and understand something of the city's history but to learn about ecological advances. Outside the church of St Adalbert on the south corner of the *Sukiennice* among the paving stones is a marble slab indicating the site where Albrecht Hohenzollern paid tribute to the King of Poland. Not far from the Town Hall Tower is another slab commemorating the oath made by Tadeusz Kościuszko. In the palace at no. 7 in 1558 the first Polish post-office was installed, functioning with admirable efficiency (a letter to Vienna took thirty-four hours). At no. 13 is a chemist's which has been there since 1403. The square also houses the most famous Polish cabaret in "Ariete's Cellar" (Piwnica pod Baranami). The luminous sign above the south side of the square gives up-to-date information on pollution levels in the old city. The square, like most of the old city, is closed to motorised traffic (residents' vehicles and public transport excluded), making both it and the surrounding streets extremely pleasant to stroll in. Those not so keen on leisurely walks might

Rynek Główny: the south wing of the *Sukiennice*.

The Statue of Adam Mickiewicz. ▶

prefer a carriage ride: carriages can be found on the west side of the square. The cafés, restaurants, shops, museums and cultural centres surrounding the square together with the historical interest of the square itself make this a delightful area to explore at length.

There are four permanent exhibitions in Rynek Główny, making this the most interesting area of the city after the Wawel hill. In the *Sukiennice* is a section of the National Museum devoted to Polish painting 1764-1900; the basement of the church of St Adalbert houses part of the Archaeological Museum and an exhibition on "The historical development of Rynek Główny,"; finally the Krzysztofory Palace (Rynek Główny, 35) and the Town Hall Tower include two exhibitions from the Cracow History Museum.

THE MONUMENT TO ADAM MICKIEWICZ

The monument to the greatest Polish romantic poet, Adam Mickiewicz, who was born in Lithuania in 1798 and died in Constantinople in 1855, was begun to mark the centenary of his birth and erected at the end of the 19th century. The city council's decision to build the monument coincided with the return of the poet's ashes, when they were laid in Wawel Cathedral. In 1890 Teodor Rygier (1841-1919) won the competition with his design for the monument. The statue stands on a high pedestal, its sides covered with allegorical figures whose significance is not altogether clear. The front of the pedestal shows the Homeland depicted as a young woman raising her arm with the figure of poetry on her left, holding a bank note in her hand. The elderly figure teaching a boy is an allegory of Science, and the young knight symbolises Patriotism. The academic style of the monument caused much controversy among young artists at the time, as the art nouveau movement was then in vogue. During the second world war the monument was dismantled and the statue of the poet, together with the allegorical figures, was taken to Germany. Fortunately it was not melted down and in 1955 when it was rediscovered it was reassembled in Cracow. The statue is an extremely popular memorial and on 24 December, the poet's name-day, all the Cracow florists pay tribute to the poet.

The eastern façade on the south wing of the *Sukiennice*.

The corner tower on the *Sukiennice*.

SUKIENNICE (THE WAREHOUSE)

The *Sukiennice*, in the middle of Rynek Główny, stands as a synthesis of architectural development in Cracow. It has been enlarged and altered over several periods, from the very earliest to the present day. In 13th century stands were set up in the centre of the square for the sale of cloth (hence the building's name). The original building dates from the reign of Casimir the Great who in 1358 ordered the construction of a large covered brick market, 100 metres long. Entrance to the building was through two large ogival doorways, one in the middle of the two main façades leading into the building. The original architect is unidentified but some fifty years later Marcin Lindintolde and the celebrated architect Mikołaj Werner worked on its reconstruction. In the 16th cen-

The western façade on the *Sukiennice*.

The neo-renaissance attic above the *Sukiennice* transept.

tury a renaissance-style attic storey was added to the structure and the building was further decorated with masks. Giovanni Maria Mosca, called il Padovano, was responsible for these alterations, carried out around 1558, while the masks have been attributed to the Florentine, Santi Gucci. Il Padovano divided the *Sukiennice* horizontally and built the staircase at the end of the building to unite the two floors. The last large-scale reconstruction of the building was between 1875 and 1879 when Tomasz Pryliński added the neogothic arcade with the capitals on the columns designed by Jan Matejko (1838-93). It was then that the upper storey was converted into a picture gallery. Between the two entrances something like a transept was constructed surmounted by a neo-renaissance attic storey. The *Sukiennice* stands right in the middle of Rynek Główny, with its extremities at the north and

The renaissance masks by Santi Gucci with the towers of the church of the Virgin Mary (Kościół Mariacki) in the background.

The towers of the church of the Virgin Mary (Kościół ▶ Mariacki) with the *Sukiennice* tower in the foreground.

south ends. Both the east and west façades are 100 metres long and extend symmetrically on either side of the entrances. The entrance on the east side, looking onto the monument to Adam Mickiewicz, appears to be the more important: above the main archway is the city's coat of arms showing a section of the city walls in red, with three towers and an open door behind which a white eagle stretches her wings. The azure shield is surmounted by a crown. Seals on the city's surviving documents bear witness to the use of this coat of arms from the 14th century. The arcades with their neo-gothic ogival arches give rhythm and focus to the lower part of the building. The iconography of the capitals deserves attention (they are the work of Jan Matejko) for although they appear at first sight to be all the same they are all different. The arcades

house cafés, tourist information offices and souvenir shops. The roof above the arcades has a stone neogothic balustrade and the attic floor above is decorated with masks. There are staircases at both ends of the building; these are covered with coffered ceilings, the one at the north end is particularly fine.

Inside the building, there is a marked contrast between the arrangement of the upper and lower floors. The ground floor is full of wooden stalls and shops selling local crafts, gifts and souvenirs from the Cracow region such as dolls in regional costume or the costumes themselves. Amateur artists display their works in the transept. The upper floor, reached from the staircase beside the main entrance, houses part of the National Museum's collection of painting and sculpture. There

12

The *Sukiennice*: the renaissance stairway designed by Padovano.

The *Sukiennice*: a window designed by T. Pryliński.

An aerial view of Rynek Główny.

are paintings by Piotr Michałowski (1800-55), Henryk Rodakowski (1823-94), Aleksander Gierymski (1850-1901), Józef Chełmoński (1849-1914), Olga Boznańska (1865-1940), and others. An entire wall in the gallery's north room is dedicated to Jan Matejko's *Hołd pruski* (a gift from the Duke of Prussia), painted in 1882: the painting is the same size as a panoramic screen. In 1939, during the Nazi occupation, the German government offered a large reward to anyone prepared to reveal the whereabouts of the hidden painting. The first work donated to the *Sukiennice* gallery was the painting of "Nero's flares" by Henryk Siemiradzki (1843-1902).

Town Hall Tower: interior.

Town Hall Tower - all that survives of the medieval Town Hall.

THE TOWN HALL TOWER
(Wieża Ratuszowa)

The tower is all that remains of Cracow's old town hall, demolished in the first quarter of the19th century. Our knowledge of the original appearance of the building derives from earlier paintings depicting events in the square such as Michał Stachowicz's painting of *Kościuszko taking the oath in Rynek Główny*, in the National museum. The surviving tower was built in about 1383 in brick with stone facing and mouldings. It is built on a square plan and more than seventy metres high with a slight inclination, some fifty-five centimetres out of true. In the 18th century, as the result of fire, the gothic spire was replaced with a small baroque dome. Although the original architecture of the building is fairly well preserved, the extraordinarily rich decorative detail, recorded in contemporary documents, is all but lost. In summer, the gallery at the top of the tower affords fine views of the old city.

Church of St Adalbert (Kościół św. Wojciecha).

THE CHURCH OF ST ADALBERT
(Kościół św. Wojciecha)

The church, romanesque in origin, dedicated to St Adalert, the patron saint of Poland and the earliest Polish saint, stands at the end of Grodzka street and is the oldest building in the Square. It was built between the 11th and 12th centuries and its limestone walls predate the *locatio civitatis* of Cracow. Built on an important trade route between Hungary and Masovia, the church also played a defensive role in the protection of the Wawel citadel to the north. In 1257 it reverted to being a strictly religious building when with the foundation of the *locatio civitatis* it became part of the building complex in around Rynek Główny. Over the centuries, mainly as a result of deposits of waste, the level of the Square became progressively higher. Today the original level of the church entrance is two metres lower than the actual pavement level. In the 15th century the walls of the church were raised and in the 17th century the construction was totally transformed. It was during this period that the church was given its baroque decoration and that the sacristy was built. The dome, covered in sheet metal and crowned with a lantern, was built in 1611. In the course of recent excavations below the foundations of the present building remains of an even earlier wooden structure have been discovered. Traditionally the church is named after St Adalbert in memory of his preaching there. The roots of christianity in Little Poland can be traced to some time before the baptism of Poland according to the wishes of Duke Mieszko II in 966. It is quite probable that even at the time of the supposed domination of the country by larger Moravia, or after 885, wooden churches were built in this area. St Adalbert, who from 983 was bishop of Prague, set out to convert the pagans of Prussia and stayed for some time at the court of Boleslaw I the Bold and later in Cracow. It is probable that he preached in a small wooden church on the site of the present building. The remains of the earlier wooden church are by no means the most ancient evidence of a sacred structure on this site, as further layers have revealed the charred remnants of an even earlier building, also of wood: perhaps a pagan temple dedicated to some early Slav deity.

During the period of expansion of the middle-class mercantile German-speaking population in Cracow, German became the exclusive language used in churches, a situation which endured with the continual expansion of the German colonies. The Polish identity of the city's population became stronger in the 15th century and the spread of printing in Polish was a decisive factor in the formation of Cracow's Polish character. The German preachers were slowly moved from the major city churches to less important ones. The parish church of St Adalbert was one of the last to abandon German, and it was not until the beginning of the 16th century that the last German sermons were preached.

ATTIC STOREY OF THE BONER PALACE

The attic storey of the Boner Palace, at no. 9 Rynek Główny, is one of the most splendid examples of the respect for 16th-century architectural detail in the historical reconstruction of a destroyed monument. The building was unhappily demolished for no good reason in the 19th century but rebuilt with meticulous care in the 1960s using original fragments, especially of the stone sculpture. The attic storey is more than eight metres in height. The lower order includes three statues of hermaphrodites, with the central one having predominantly female attributes. Above these are two masks of satyrs and four linked griffins, these in turn surmounted by three stone balls. In 1606 the wedding banquet of Marina Mniszech and the false Demetrius took place in the Boner palace. It was Demetrius who pretended to be the son of Ivan the Terrible.

The attic storey on the Boner Palace with the dome of the church of St Adalbert (Kościół św. Wojciecha).

Church of the Virgin Mary (Kościół Mariacki) - dedicated to the Assumption of Mary.

THE CHURCH OF THE VIRGIN MARY (Kościół Mariacki)

The gothic church dedicated to the Assumption of the Virgin Mary, usually referred to as the church of the Virgin Mary, is the most significant monument in the area of Rynek Główny. For centuries it was the most important church in the city, frequented by the merchant classes, while the Cathedral on Wawel was officially the main diocesan church. It was built on the site of a romanesque church founded at the beginning of the 13th century by Bishop Iwo Odrowaz; now only its irregular position in relation to the plan of Rynek Główny remind us of the earlier construction. It is built entirely of hand-made bricks on a basilican plan with a high central nave and two lower side aisles. The main body of the church was built between 1350 and 1397 when the architect Mikołaj Werner finished the

ceiling above the nave. It took the entire 15th century to complete the structure with the erection of the towers, the addition of the chapels and the completion of the ceilings. The higher gothic spire dates from 1478 and the golden crown, symbol of the Virgin as Queen of Poland, was added in 1666. The dome on the lower tower was finished in the 16th century. Inside the lower tower, the belfry, are five bells; the largest, known as *Półzygmunt* (the half Sigismund) was founded in 1438. A popular anecdote has it that the bell was carried to the top of the tower by the son of the Voivode of Masovia, Stanisław Ciołek , famous for his athletic feats. The higher tower has served as a watchtower since the middle ages. In the past the guards were obliged to raise the alarm in the case of fire or of attack by the enemy. Today the firemen on duty must be vigilant in the prevention of fire but have also to play on the hour a musical phrase *hejnał mariacki*.

Hejnał is a word of Hungarian origin meaning *morning,* the phrase might then be interpreted as "awake", a sort of military reveille to wake the town, a theory reinforced by the sprightly tune. Today it is not only heard in the morning but divides the day: every hour a trumpeter sounds the *hejnał* to the points of the compass and at midday Radio 1 Poland broadcasts the tune throughout Poland; radio equipment was first installed in the tower in 1926. The sound of this tune, echoing as it has done for years among the old city walls around the church gives the old quarter a character that is quite unique. Naturally the *hejnał* is also linked to a legend, like so much in old Cracow. During the Tartar invasions a watchman, having sighted the enemy approaching, began to sound the tune but was shot in the throat by a Tartar arrow, at which point the alarm abruptly ceased (the *hejnał mariacki*.still appears to end half way through the phrase). Although the watchman died the people of Cracow were able to repel the attack and after pursuing the enemy captured some rich booty.

The decoration of the church interior, its paintings and stained glass windows are in a range of styles: from the gothic to 19th-century revival, from the baroque to liberty. The most remarkable object in the church is the altarpiece by Weit Stoss. There are also some marvellous pieces of sculpture in wood and stone from a variety of periods: crucifixes, tombs, altars. The Basilica treasury contains Cracowian goldsmiths' work and liturgical vestments, and has fine 17th-century baroque fittings in which the works are displayed (this was Cracow's earliest museum).

The church façade with its asymmetrical towers.

The church of the Virgin Mary
(Kościół Mariacki).

The Weit Stoss altar in the church of ▶
the Virgin Mary (Kościół Mariacki),
considered one of the finest piece of
late-gothic sculpture.

THE FAÇADE OF THE CHURCH OF THE VIRGIN MARY

The church towers, begun in the 15th century, arouse our curiosity today because of the apparent architectural jest incorporated in their construction. At their bases they appear to have been planned symmetrically, with the lower floors provided with the same elements. The small differences at this level are the result of restoration. The north tower, the higher one, has eight floors of equal height while the south tower from the seventh floor up, has floors of increasing height as though attempting to overtake the other one. The size of the windows in both towers remains the same. The renaissance dome on the lower tower is at the same height as the ninth floor of the other tower, which at this level changes from a square plan to an octagonal one, terminating in a gothic spire, surrounded by a crown of smaller spires. And so the tower that seemed so eager to reach the heavens was forestalled ....and here too hangs a tale. The builders of the towers were two brothers who were eager to outdo each other, and each strove to make his own tower the higher. The elder, when he had finished the north tower, murdered his brother to prevent his finishing the south tower. Remorse however soured his success. After a public confession of his crime he committed suicide by leaping from a high window of his own tower. His knife, the fatal weapon, was displayed as a sign of atonement at the entrance to the *Sukiennice,* where it is still to be seen today.

THE ALTAR BY WEIT STOSS

Weit Stoss (Wit Stosw), born in Nuremberg, arrived in Cracow in 1477 having been commissioned by the city's merchants to carve the altarpiece for the church of the Virgin Mary. The work, a monumental wooden polyptych, is considered one of the finest pieces of European late-gothic sculpture. Carved in limewood it is made up of a central section with four wings; the two fixed ones can only be admired when the two central mobile ones are closed. The lower part of the central panel depicts the *Dormition of the Virgin with the Apostles* while the upper section is devoted to the *Assumption*. A carved baldachin above the central panel frames the scene of the *Coronation of the Virgin*

Page 24: the *Dormition* of *the Virgin* and the *Assumption* ▶
(central panel of the Weit Stoss altar).
Page 25: one of the scenes from the wings of the altar ▶
showing the *Resurrection* and the stone *Crucifix*,
by Weit Stoss in the south aisle of the church of the
Virgin Mary (Kościół Mariacki).

by the Holy Trinity. The mobile wings depict the *Annunciation*, the *Nativity*, the *Adoration of the Magi*, the *Resurrection*, the *Ascension* and *Pentecost*. The predella panel is carved with the *Tree of Jesse* to show the genealogy of the Virgin. The figures in the central panel are larger than life-size, indeed the figure of St Peter supporting the body of the Virgin is 280 cm high.

23

Plac Mariacki, the square in front of the church of St Barbara.

PLAC MARIACKI
(St Mary's Square)

Enclosed between the palaces on the east side of the adjacent Rynek Główny and the churches of the Virgin Mary and St Barbara, St Mary's Square is built on the site of the old parish cemetery. The last burials took place in the 18th century, as in the early 19th century the cemetery was moved. The square, called *Plac Mariacki*, is attractive both on account of its architectural setting and because of its unusual stillness, in marked contrast to the bustle of Rynek Główny. The beauty of the square has attracted film directors, such as M. Anderson who chose it to shoot several scenes of his film *The goldsmith's workshop*, taken from the book of the same name by Karol Wojtyła. The walls of the churches of the Virgin Mary and St Barbara bear epitaphs to Cracow merchants, with inscriptions in both Latin and Polish, the earliest dating to the 16th century. A memorial plaque on one of the buildings records how Stanislao Wyspianski wrote one of his most important pieces *Wesele* (The Wedding) when living here. The attractive fountain in the middle of the square was commissioned by Cracow craftsmen. As St Mary's square is completely enclosed by high buildings it has extraordinary acoustic properties, as if it were a deep well: even the softest whisper is audible. The *hejnał* tune is heard here to perfection when it is played in a southerly direction.

The entrance to the church of St Barbara.

Ogrójec at the entrance to the church of St Barbara.

THE CHURCH OF ST BARBARA

Tradition has it that the Church of St Barbara, founded in 1362 by Mikołaj Wierzynek, was built with the bricks left over from the Church of the Virgin Mary. It became a funerary chapel. In the second half of the 16th century it became the first Jesuit centre in Cracow. In the north wall of the church there is a memorial plaque to Jakub Wujek, of the Society of Jesus, who was responsible for the first translation of the Bible into Polish, a splendid work published in 1599 and still used by the Church. The church interior is decorated according to the taste of the 17th century, when the last restoration work was carried out.

OGRÓJEC

At the entrance to the Church of St Barbara, in the *Ogrójec* (Gethsemane) Chapel, is a sculpture, attributed by some to Weit Stoss, of *The Agony in the Garden*. The clumsy rendering of the large sandstone figures does not inspire confidence in the attribution to the master. The work is protected by an arched loggia built between 1488 and 1518 with elegant iron gates. The high arches and the short twisted columns reflect the typical uneasiness of late-medieval architecture.

THE FOUNTAIN STATUE

The perfect proportions of the graceful figure of the rather sad youth with a turban, bent over the fountain in St Mary's Square, strongly suggest the hand of Weit Stoss. The work is however a bronze copy cast by Cracow craftsmen in 1958. The smaller original is included in the surround of the main section of the altarpiece in the Church of the Virgin Mary. It is placed on the right in the middle panel, close to the lower edge in the scene of the Resurrection. The size and position of the altarpiece makes it difficult to see the figure clearly without the aid of binoculars. The copy of the statue, however, when viewed in broad daylight provides a fine illustration of the typical features of the style of Weit Stoss.

The east side of Plac Mały Rynek.

THE OLD CITY

MAŁY RYNEK (The small Market Square)

A charming passage, near the Ogrójec, links St Mary's Square to the small *Mały Rynek*. This small square appears on the city maps as early as 1257 and previously served as an auxiliary market. For many years only meat and salami were sold but at the beginning of the 19th century fruit also appeared. The square, sloping towards the south, is lined on its east side with a row of medieval buildings. Opposite these, on the west side is the church of St Barbara complex. In summer the square becomes a large open-air café filled with colourful umbrellas; a perfect place to rest and enjoy the city's architectural heritage. On cold, wet days the smart cafés and small restaurants offer the perfect retreat. In 1661 in the Szober house at no. 6 (*kamienica Szoberowska*) the first Polish periodical was founded: the weekly *Polish Mercury*, edited by Jan Aleksander Gorczyn. It appeared as part of the reform programme initiated by King John Casimir and his wife Maria Ludovica. 100-250 copies were printed but it only lasted for forty-one weeks as the reform programme failed and the King was forced to abdicate. Following Szpitalna street, leading out of the square we reach św. Ducha (Holy Spirit Square) where there once stood a church and hospital of the same name, destroyed in the second half of the 19th century. The demolition of the hospital, founded in the 13th century by the Canons Regular of the Holy Spirit, from which the square derives its name, was a tremendous loss to all those who valued the city's historical past. There are still two buildings of interest today however: the austere gothic architecture of the church of St Cross contrasting with the decorative exuberance of the Juliusz Słowacki Theatre.

The gothic vaulting in the St Cross church
(Kościół św. Krzyża).

CHURCH OF ST CROSS (Kościół św. Krzyża)

Built near the city walls the Church of St Cross in part suggests a fortified structure. Although begun in 1300 the main building was raised some years later. It has a nave with no side aisles and the façade fronts a solid square tower surmounted by a spire covered in tiles, an extremely unusual feature on churches in Cracow. On the presbytery side of the church we can see a stretch of stone wall with the remains of loopholes. The rich interior of the church offers a surprising contrast to its external severity. A single column in the centre of the nave supports a network of fan-vaulting. This feature, like the tiles covering the spire, is also unique to this church. The walls are covered with fine paintings; the oldest, dating to 1420 and showing *The Agony in the Garden,* is in the chapel. The walls are covered with renaissance grotesque decoration, with plant motifs in

the nave and presbytery (partly reconstructed); the leaf, flower and fruit motifs are splendid in their variety. The fresco work has been attributed to Stanisław Samostrelnik, a monk from the Mogiła convent, supposedly the first Polish painter to adopt the renaissance style. His date of birth is uncertain but believed to be about 1490. He entered the Cistercian convent as a young man and in 1514, while travelling in Hungary as chaplain to the chancellor K. Szydłowiecki, he first encountered Italian renaissance painting which had become popular in the lands of Pannonia. He never shed his links with the so-called "school of Cracow", and retained many late-gothic elements in his style. He died in Cracow in 1541, having also gained a reputation as a miniaturist both at court and among rich private patrons. His most important works are the miniature prayer books for King Sigismund and Queen Bona Sforza, together with the fresco decoration of the church and Cistercian convent at Mogiła near Cracow (now in the Nowa Huta district). The presence of grotesque work together with the coat of arms of Piotr Tomicki, Samostrzelnik's patron, in the Mogiła convent remove any doubts about the attribution to him of the decoration in the Church of the St Cross. The church also has a fine bronze font of 1423 from the workshop of Jan Fredenthal. The late-gothic wooden choir stalls bear witness to the extremely high quality of inlay-work in Cracow in the 15th century. The church of St Cross was for some time the hospital chapel but at the end of the last century was adopted by the actors of Cracow as their own church. Among others who worshipped there was Helena Modrzejewska (1840-1909), a celebrated actress who worked in both Poland and America, where she was known as Helena Modjeska. Today the church's association with actors continues on account of the neighbouring Juliusz Słowacki Theatre. In 1995 restoration work began on the renaissance frescoes which means that visiting the church is restricted.

The St Cross (Kościół św. Krzyża) tower.

The Juliusz Słowacki Theatre

Music, Opera and Operetta: sculpture surmounting the ▶
right bay on the theatre façade.

THE JULIUSZ SŁOVACKI THEATRE

The Juliusz Słowacki Theatre was built between 1890 and 1893 as the new city theatre and was considered to have one of the most technically advanced stages in the world. Cracow in the 19th century was, and indeed modern Cracow still is, a city in which artists were particularly favoured. The first electricity plant in the city was destined for the exclusive use of the theatre and although now no longer in use, situated behind the theatre, it is a fine example of the technical achievements of the late 19th century.

The theatre's first production in October 1893 brought together Polish cultural figures from all over the world. Scientists joined with artists of all kinds throughout Poland to demonstrate their solidarity in a nation at that time divided by three occupying powers. The new theatre was intended to replace the old theatre in Plac Szczepański, but resulted in the formation of two excellent companies: the City Theatre Company and the other based on the old theatre. Originally the new theatre was to be named after Count Aleksander Fredro, a playwright who lived between 1793 and 1876 and whose works include *Zemsta* (Revenge) and *Śluby panieńskie* (The Girl's Vows), anti-romantic satires which have become part of the classical Polish repertory. Fedro's bust stands outside the theatre entrance. A change in taste and the success of the art-nouveau movement led to the theatre being named after the great romantic poet Juliusz Słowacki (1809-49) rather than Fredro. The building was designed by the Cracowian architect Jan Zawiejski (1854-1922) who was strongly influenced by the Opera in Paris, built between 1861 and 1875. When the new theatre opened in Cracow, Charles Garnier, the architect of the Opera, sent Zawiejski a letter of congratulation.

33

The bust of Aleksander Fredro in the small square in front of the theatre.

The theatre can house an audience of more than 920 and has exceptionally good acoustics which were adjusted during the construction by a committee composed of, among others, representatives from the Conservatory. Experts maintain that Cracow is the best Polish city for theatre, for while there are more of them in Warsaw Cracow's theatrical productions are of higher quality. It was here that Helena Modrzejewska began her career, and Konrad Swinarski and Tadeusz Kantor also performed in this theatre. During the nazi occupation, when all artistic activity was forbidden, the secret Rhapsodic Theatre was started in Cracow, with Karol Wojtyła, the future John Paul II, among its actors. One of the most important dates in the history of the Polish theatre was the first performance on 16 March 1901 of Stanisław Wyspiański's *Wesele* (The Wedding) at the Juliusz Słowacki Theatre.

The theatre façade is extraordinary in the richness of its sculptural decoration. The largest groups of figures are at the extremities of the façade above the cornice with Poetry, Tragedy and Comedy on the left by Tadeusz Błotnicki; and Music, Operetta and Opera on the right by Alfred Daun. In the centre of the building are a male and female figure in noble dress and in dancing positions in a group entitled "And now for a Polonaise!" sculpted by Michał Korpala (they represent Taddeus and Sophie, the main characters in Adam Mickiewicz's *Taddeus*). Between the two figures engraved on a red marble slab in gold letters is the inscription: Cracow's gift to the national heritage. The male busts on the projecting wing façades represent Joy and Sorrow and are the work of Mieczysław Zawiejski , the architect's brother, who died while still a young man. The architectural details are in harmony with traditional Cracow

The pair of figures "And now for a Polonaise!"

The ring of masks around the base of the theatre dome.

motifs as for example, the use of large masks, like those on the *Sukiennice*. These masks run all around the base of the theatre dome, which is itself a remarkable feature. It is the interplay of architectural elements of various styles and periods, the eclectic element which is the predominant feature of Jan Zawiejski's design even though its boldness and functionalism prefigure the Liberty style. Although built comparatively recently the theatre is of great importance in Cracow's history. The public attending the first performances there would jestingly remark " the dragon swallowed a pearl". The various rooms perfectly reflect the taste of the period and are its finest expression. Particularly splendid is the curtain painted by Henryk Siemiradzki (1834-1902), who worked in Paris and Munich and returned to his native Poland to found the National Museum with the donation of one of his paintings.

◀ St Florian's Gate: the north side.

Klastorek, the Little Monastery, now the
Czartoryskich Museum.

BRAMA FLORIAŃSKA (St Florian's Gate)

In the 15th century the historic centre of Cracow was surrounded by a moat and by a double walls with square and circular towers: eight gates led into the city. Today some traces of the fortifications survive including sections of the wall and the interesting St Florian's gate. In the park to the north of the gate stands the *Barbakan* - a gothic structure built in defence of the city's main entrance. St Florian's Gate, which controlled the main access to city, is first mentioned in 1307 and was dedicated to the city's patron saint whose relics reached Cracow in 1184. At the beginning of the 14th century the square stone tower was built above the gate, in the same style as the original, while the top of the tower was added in the 16th century. Remains of the old city wall are visible on both sides of the gate together with the Carpenters' Tower and the Joiners' Tower. Today the tower is a favourite exhibiting space for local artists, mostly amateurs or students from the Art School, who enjoy the chance of augmenting their modest incomes by selling a few paintings. Often these works, although produced for money, display genuine talent especially in the copying of Old Masters. Inside the gothic archway is a tabernacle with a painting of the Virgin. On the north side is the white eagle (sculpted on a design of Jan Matejko), while on the south side is a baroque low-relief depicting St Florian as patron saint of the Fire Brigade, extinguishing a fire.

THE PRINCES' CZARTORYSKI MUSEUM

Walking along the city walls from St Florian's Gate to the west at no.15 ulica Pijarska, beside the 16th-century Arsenal, is the neo-gothic *Muzeum książąt Czartoryskich* (now part of the National Museum). This museum has had a very troubled history. It houses paintings and sculptures, objets d'art, documents

37

◄ Czartoryskich Museum: hussars' armour.

◄ Czartoryskich Museum: a breastplate in the armour collection.

Royal mementoes: in the background a series of miniatures with portraits of the family of King Sigismund I by Lucas Cranach the Younger.

and a library. All the works collected by the Czartoryski family from the middle of the 18th century were exhibited in 1800 in Puławy, in the building known as the Temple of Sibyl, built especially to house the collection and therefore the first museum of its kind in Poland. It was a gesture designed to stir the country's historical imagination and to revive hope in the resurgence of the Polish state. But with the failure of the November uprising the museum received a severe blow: the Russians condemned Prince Adam Jerzy Czartoryski to death for his leading role in the insurrection and issued a writ for the confiscation of all his property. The united efforts of his family and their servants led to a large part of the collection being hidden and removed to Paris, where it remained for several decades. When Prince Władysław Czartoryski wanted to bring the collection back to Cracow he bought the buildings in ulica Pijarska and after re-

construction work opened the museum there. In 1936, according to a contemporary guide, the museum contained some 70,000 books, 5,000 manuscripts, 5,000 volumes of family archives, 1,311 diplomas and certificates, 2,500 maps and atlases, 7,150 ancient and modern objets d'art, 450 paintings, 970 prehistoric fragments, 1,750 ancient Greek, Roman and Islamic pieces, 2,230 drawings and some 19,000 prints. About a third of the exhibits came from the Puławy collection. During the war part of this treasure was lost including the *a portrait study* by Raphael. In 1950 the museum became State property. Among the most outstanding works in the collection are the *Portrait of a Young Woman with an Ermine* by Leonardo da Vinci and a *Landscape with the Good Samaritan* by Rembrandt van Rijn.

Leonardo's *Portrait of a Young Woman with an Ermine*, his most famous female portrait together with

39

◀ *Portrait of a Young Woman with an Ermine* by Leonardo da Vinci.

Czartoryskich Museum: renaissance portraits.

the *Mona Lisa*, was painted in about 1492. The subject of the portrait is probably Cecilia Gallerani, a lady-in-waiting at the Milanese court and the lover of Ludovico Sforza il Moro. The painting was bought by the Czartoryski in Italy and was the pride of the Puławy collection. For some years it was kept in the Hôtel Lambert, Paris. It has been in Cracow for 120 years and has left the city three times: during the first world war when the Czartoryski transferred it to Dresden; during the second world war when it was plundered by the Germans; and in 1992 when, because it had been painted in 1492, it was sent to New York as part of the exhibition in celebration of Columbus. The ermine in the arms of the beautiful Cecilia, sometimes identified as a weasel, alludes to Ludovico il Moro who was nick-named the *Ermellino* or the ermine.

The *Landscape with the Good Samaritan*, also known as the *Landscape before the Storm*, painted in 1638, is the most remarkable work by Rembrandt in the Polish collections. It depicts a landscape with figures hidden in the shade of trees that create, to the right of the painting, a scene showing the episode from St Luke's gospel (10,30-37). The work was bought for the Czartoryski by the French painter Jan Piotr Norblin in 1717 and became part of the Puawy collection, having previously been in the Hague and Paris. The painting is in oil on an oak panel and measures 46.5 x 66 cm.

One of the rooms devoted to painting.

Landscape with the Good Samaritan by Rembrandt van Rijn.

Collection of Sacred Art from the Szołayski Palace, part of the National Museum : *Polyptych of the life of St John the Almsgiver.*

KAMIENICA SZOŁAYSKICH

The Szołayski palace, at no. 9 plac Szołayskich, a square opening off the west side of Rynek Główny, houses a collection of Polish painting and sculpture and is also part of the National Museum. In 1904 Adam and Włodzimierz Szołayscy, members of an old Cracow family, left the National Museum their home to house the Japanese collection of Feliks Jasieński-Mangha (in 1994 the collection was moved to the modern pavilion on the right bank of the Vistula by Andrzej Wajda and Krystyna Zachwatowicz). The Szołayski museum includes a collection of painting and sculpture largely executed by members of guilds and corporations, and representative of medieval and renaissance trends in Polish art. The works are predominantly religious, as they were throughout Europe at this time when the power and influence of the Catholic Church were unchallenged. Because of the religious content of the works displayed in the *kamienica Szołayskich* it is often referred to as the Museum of Sacred Art.

THE POLYPTYCH OF ST JOHN THE ALMSGIVER

The most outstanding piece in the Szołayski museum is the 16th-century polyptych depicting the miraculous life of St John the Almsgiver, an extremely rare subject in Polish painting as St John has scant popular devotion. John was Patriarch of Alexandria in the 7th century. His cult, widespread in the countries of the Middle East, reached the Vistula through the work of Mikołaj Lanckoronski, of the noble Zadora family. In 1501 Mikołaj Lanckoroński took part in a diplomatic mission to Constantinople. Staying in Hungary on the outward journey, he learnt of the cult of St John which was then spreading in Pannonia after his relics had been given to the King of Hungary Mathias Corvinus by the Turkish Sultan, Bajazet. As Lanckoronski continued his journey south he learnt more of the saint's cult in the near east. He was so impressed by accounts of the saint's life and by the exotic places associated with his name that on his return to Cracow he commissioned local artists to paint an altarpiece devoted to St

John. The altarpiece is composed of five wooden panels, painted in tempera. The central panel depicts the Patriarch distributing alms and is flanked by two panels on each side, each containing two scenes. The outer sections show scenes from the eremetical life while the inner four show scenes from the life of St John the Almsgiver; one taking place at his tomb depicts a post-mortem miracle. The painter, known as the "Master of the St John the Almsgiver Polyptych", is sometimes identified with Jan Goraj or with Joachim Libnaw from Droszów, but lack of documentary evidence makes a definitive attribution impossible.

THE DĘBNO HOLY TRINITY

The *Holy Trinity*, painted in tempera with a gold ground on panel, is a large altarpiece (205 x 150 cm) executed circa 1520 for the parish church of Dębno near Wojnicz (some 60 km east of Cracow). It was commissioned by a knight, Jakub Dębiński, lord of Dębno from 1489 to 1524. It is a votive offering typical of its time. The composition shows the Father enthroned supporting the arms of the Cross on which His Son is crucified. The dove, symbol of the Holy Spirit, appears above the head of Christ. Members of the donor's family kneel in adoration at the bottom of the painting: to the right of Christ are Jakub Dębiński of the Odrowąż family and his sons, while to the left are his wife, of the Leliwa family, and his daughters. This style of presenting the donors is typical of votive painting in Little Poland.

◀ *Polyptych of the life of St John the Almsgiver:* central panel.

Polyptych of the life of St John the Almsgiver: scene from the life of the Patriarch.

Polyptych of the life of St John the Almsgiver:
a post-mortem miracle.

The Holy Trinity by Dębno. ▶

THE ALTAR OF THE DOMINICANS

In the 1430s the beginnings of the Cracow school of painting are first discernible; this school is sometimes referred to as the Cracow-Sącz school or, more correctly as the school of Little Poland. It developed from the circle of artists belonging to the painters' guild, founded as an independent body in 1404, and it exerted considerable influence on Polish, Silesian and Slovakian painting as well as on the painting of Northern Hungary. The earliest example of the school is the painting known as the Epitaph of Wirzbięta of Branice, while its greatest exponent, when the style had reached its fullest development away from traditional painting, was the "Master of the Passion of the Dominicans", an unidentified Cracowian painter active in the 15th century. Between 1460 and 1465 he painted twelve paintings for the altarpiece in the Dominican church, arranged on the mobile wings of a polyptych. The style and composition of the paintings change according to where they were to be placed. The paintings inside the wings, nearly always exposed to the faithful, were given a greater monumentality and followed more traditional trends in the treatment of the figures on a gold ground, typical of painting in Cracow in the 15th century. The painting of the reverse side (only visible when the altarpiece is closed) reflect a more innovative style in the treatment of the figures, closer to renaissance ideals; for the first time the gold ground is replaced with a landscape. The fragments of the Passion illustrated in the photographs come from the inner side of the wings.

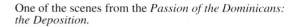

One of the scenes from the *Passion of the Dominicans: the Deposition.*

THE EPITAPH OF
GRZEGORZ WIRZBĘTA OF BRANICE

This is the work of an unidentified Cracowian painter, active in the first half of the 15th century, painted in tempera on panel (91 x 74 cm) circa 1425 in commemoration of Grzegorz Wirzbięta of Branice. It was intended for the parish church of Ruszcza, founded by Wirzbięta. The painting depicts an armed knight kneeling in front of the Virgin and Child. St Gregory, the patron saint of the dead man, also appears in the painting placing his hand on his shoulder in a protective gesture. The figures are painted in hierarchical proportion so that the size of the Virgin and of St Gregory is disproportionate to that of the tiny Wirzbięta. His identity is made clear by the presence of the coats of arms of the "Grifo" and the "Leliwa" at the bottom of the painting, as well as by the inscription in gold letters on the wooden frame. The work, while anticipating the new manner of the school of Cracow, still shows traces of the influence of Bohemian painting apparent in Little Poland until later in the 15th century when it became superseded by the ascendancy of the Cracow Painters' Guild.

THE MICHAŁ LENCZ TRIPTYCH

Michał Lencz of Kitzingen came to live in Cracow in 1507 and died there in 1523. He was initially commissioned by King Sigismund to paint the rooms in Wawel castle. In 1516 he went into the service of Bishop Jan Konarski, and was selected to paint the altarpiece for the funerary chapel of his patron. He chose to paint a triptych divided into five panels. The central section shows the *Dormition of the Virgin* set in a contemporary house, probably of a well-to-do merchant. Lencz's painting combines certain minor characteristics of the Cracow school with an obvious debt to Albrecht Dürer and Lucas Cranach the Elder. His use of the cold colours found in German renaissance painting distances this work from those by painters of the Cracow school.

The Epitaph of Grzegorz Wirzbięta of Branice.

48

The Michał Lencz altarpiece

THE BEAUTIFUL MADONNA

There are numerous examples of medieval sculpture carved in Cracow, and one of the most important pieces is the Krużlowa *Mother and Child*. This poly-chrome statue, 118 cm high, came from the parish church in Krużlowa to the National Museum in 1899. It is representative of works known as "Beautiful Madonnas" which first appeared in French stone statu-ary and later in wooden sculpture in central Europe.

49

One of the scenes from the *Passion of the Dominicans: the Entombment.*

The beautiful Madonna from Krużlowa.

Following page: the *Collegium Maius.*

The characteristic feature of all these pieces is the curve of the Madonna's body into an "S" shape. The treatment of the drapery and the Mother's tender idealised expression suggest that the Krużlowa Madonna was carved circa 1400; the *Madonna z Krużlowej* is the most beautiful piece of sculpture in the Szołayski museum.

COLLEGIUM MAIUS

After leaving the Szołayski museum and following ulica Jagiellońska we reach one of the oldest University buildings in the world. The *Collegium Maius*, dating from 1400, is now the Historic Museum of the Jagiellonian University; its more magnificent rooms are used for special celebrations. The Jagiellonian University grew out of the Cracow

Entrance to the University garden.

Following page: the rooms of the original University library.

Academy, founded in 1364 by King Casimir the Great; it was, after Prague, the most important University in central Europe. With the death of Casimir in 1370 the University failed to develop successfully under Casimir's successor, Louis d'Anjou. The Academy did however receive valuable support from Louis' daughter, Jadwiga, who left all her jewels for its modernisation. The University's greatest patron then became King Wladyslaw Jagiello, whose Lithuanian name has been given to it ever since. The University holds a special place in Polish history, as its activity has remained uninterrupted since its foundation despite various attempts at persecution and periods of clandestine operations; in this it can be compared to the unbroken tradition of the Catholic Church in Poland. Today the *Uniwersytet Jagielloński* continues to exert a strong in-

Below left: the courtyard of the *Collegium Maius;*
below right: the votive stone of the Jerusalem Hostel

Stuba Communis or the Hall.

The Jagiellonian University: Lecture Room. ▶

fluence on Cracowian cultural life.

The *Collegium Maius* we see today is the reconstruction of a building which in 1400 stood on the corner of św. Anny and Jagiellońska and which was purchased by King Jagiello as a gift to the Academy. In the reconstruction and expansion of the building which immediately followed, the Hall (*Stuba Communis*) was built, complete with the reader's chair, and now appears on the east façade as a projecting tower. The alterations to the building were finished in the early 16th century: it emerged as a quadrilateral with a large inner courtyard with a cloistered walk with gothic arches, similar to the Wawel castle courtyard, built only a few years later but closer to the renaissance in style. The atmosphere in the University courtyard transports us back to the days when Nicholas Copernicus taught astronomy at the Collegium Maius. Jan Kochanowski also studied here before gaining renown as a poet; legend has it that Doctor Faust also studied here. Goethe certainly stayed in Cracow before writing his *Faust*, and there is a commemorative plaque on the house he stayed in, where ulica

Sławkowska meets Rynek Główny. Other architectural features worth noticing are the decorative surrounds of the doorways and the stone commemorating the construction of the "Jerusalem" hostel. The stone is carved like a votive offering. Cardinal Zbigniew Oleśnicki kneels before the Virgin offering her a model of the hostel, built in reparation for an unfulfilled promise to go on pilgrimage to Jerusalem. The Cardinal's political interests led to his postponing his departure until he finally decided to build the University hostel. The conversion of such vows into the realisation of public works was by no means rare in the 15th century. The courtyard leads into the reception rooms and to the splendid apartments devoted to the museum. The rich decoration and architectural detail of these rooms not only reflect generous Jagiellonian patronage but also the happy discovery of a hidden Magyar treasure containing 2,508 pieces of Hungarian gold coin and rings, precious stones and pearls of the same value. Among these was an extremely rare black diamond and a pearl necklace mounted in gold, together with thirteen sapphires and rubies.

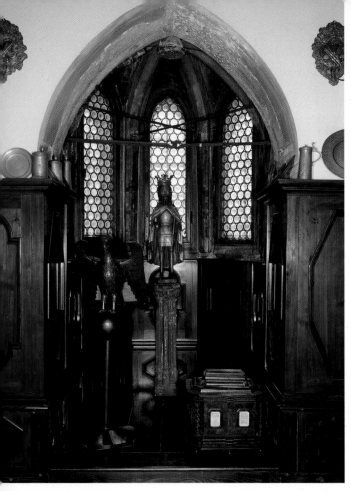

Statue of Casimir the Great in the small tribune of the *Stuba Communis*.

Collegium Maius: detail of the *Stuba Communis*.

15th-and 16th-century astronomical instruments. ▶

MUZEUM DZIEJÓW UNIWERSYTETU JAGIELLOŃSKIEGO

The Historic Museum of the Jagiellonian University was founded to preserve documents relating to the history of the University as well as works of art, for the most part produced by local artists. The most precious pieces in the collection are the medieval insignia of the University rector, togas and other ceremonial robes together with alchemical and astronomical instruments. Among these is a *mappamundi* of 1510, the first to indicate America (*America terra noviter reperta*). On the ground floor we can visit the lecturing rooms (Galeno's *lectorium*, for example, where Copernicus came to hear the lectures given by Wojciech of Brudzewo). On the first floor are the reception rooms of the Cracow Athenaeum: *Libraria*, *Stuba Communis* and the Jagiellonian Hall. The *Stuba Communis* was where the University masters ate their meals until the end of the 18th century; it is now only used for special occasions such as the election of the

rector or for important receptions. The Jagiellonian Hall, the largest room in the University, is in itself a wonderful illustration of the University's history. The walls are decorated with portraits of benefactors and patrons of the Athenaeum; there is a coffered ceiling and stalls for the masters. The renaissance doorway bears the motto: *Plus ratio quam vis* (Reason is greater than strength). Honorary degrees are conferred in the Hall.

COLLEGIUM NOVUM

In the second half of the 19th century the University of Cracow made some notable advances in the scientific field, including the liquefaction of oxygen in 1883 by Karol Olszewski and Zygmunt Wróblewski. On the site of the Jerusalem hostel, demolished in the cause of modernisation, the *Collegium Novum* was built after the design of Feliks Księżarski. The building contains the Rector's rooms and the principle offices of the

Collegium Novum, home of the Rector of the Jagiellonian University.

The view over *Planty* from the windows of Wawel Castle. ▶

Athenaeum. The statue of Copernicus stands on the grass just outside the building. It was moved there during the restoration of the 15th-century aspects of the *Collegium Novum,* the largest of the University buildings in Poland to incorporate a courtyard in the original design.

PLANTY

The "Old City" is surrounded by a green belt of public gardens, known as Planty, built on an ellipsoidal plan, the only example of its kind in the world. The bronze plaques along the avenues indicate the 15th- and 16th-century sites of the towers that protected the city and that together with the city walls were demolished to create the Planty. Medieval chroniclers when describing Cracow refer to its having the shape of a lute. Today, from the air, this outline is still visible: the oblong "sound box" encloses the Rynek Główny, area and, following along ulica Grodza the outline of that part of the old city the line narrows in the neck of a griffin, its head being formed by the Royal Castle of Wawel. The city's unusual outline is enhanced by the surrounding green belt of the public gardens.

Aerial view of Wawel Hill.

WAWEL HILL

The oldest views of Cracow show a city clustered at the bottom of a hill. The Hill has always been a dominating element in the city, looking over the Vistula. There was originally a straight drop from the summit of the hill to the river, with a wall of Jurassic limestone. From as early as Palaeolithic times, men lived in the caves carved by the river water into the rock. Archaeological excavations have revealed that in the 6th century a fortified settlement existed at the top of the hill (228 metres) and there are traces of a Christian church dating from the 9th century. The biography of St Methodius, Archbishop of Greater Moravia, written in 885 includes the following extract: "a very powerful pagan prince who reigned *na Wisle* (on the Vistula) had the custom of persecuting Christians and subjecting them to frequent attacks. Methodius sent him a messenger who reported: 'it would be better for you, my son, to offer yourself for baptism in your own land rather than to be baptised by force, as a prisoner in a strange land. When that moment comes you will remember me.' And that is what happened" (The *Legend of St Methodius* was translated into Polish from ancient ecclesiastical Slav by Tadeusz Lehr-Spławiński). The compulsory baptism of the Vislani ruler explains the origins of the foundations, of the fragments of wall and of the crypt, all belonging to pre-Roman buildings

discovered in the course of excavations. The remains and progressive juxtaposition of a variety of structures, some of them very early, make this an architectural complex of incomparable historic and artistic value. In the 19th century Wawel was called the Polish Acropolis, a phrase which not only reflects the Poles' patriotic fervour but is also a good description of the role played by Wawel Hill in the country's cultural history.

THE CASTLE

The remains of a building discovered during excavations are thought to be the earliest castle constructed on Wawel Hill. It was of stone and was built between the 10th and 11th centuries. At the beginning of the 12th century a romanesque fortified castle stood on the hill, while the first gothic building, fragments of which have been incorporated into later constructions, was built by Wladyslaw the Short who sought to strengthen Cracow's role as a capital city. His son Casimir the Great (1333-70), responsible for the construction of a large number of castles in Poland in the 14th century, built an impressive gothic castle on the hill of which only the tower *Kurza Stopka* (Chicken's foot) remains. Beside it stands the gothic pavilion with a large terrace: this was added during the reign of Jadwiga of Anjou and Wladyslaw Jagiello as part of the alterations made to Casimir's building. The most notable changes were made at the beginning of the 16th century, when, after the disastrous fire of 1499, King Alexander and his son Sigismund undertook the reconstruction of the castle in the renaissance style. This

The renaissance Castle of Wawel.

◀ Wawel: the Cathedral and the castle.

The *Kurza Stopka* (Chicken's foot Tower).

building too was damaged by fire; in the reconstruction work which followed, some of the rooms were enriched with baroque decoration. When the court was transferred to Warsaw the castle suffered a period of decline. The loss of Poland's independence and her occupation meant that the castle served as an Austrian garrison which caused it considerable damage. Efforts were later made to restore the castle, the symbol of independent Poland, to its former dignity. The dedication of groups of citizens led to the reconstruction of the Wawel buildings in 1905, and under Franz Josef restoration of the monumental interiors was begun. After the first world war a museum was opened in the castle: *Państwowe Zbiory Sztuki na Wawelu* (State Art Collection).

The Thieves' Tower.

The courtyard of Wawel Castle.

THE COURTYARD OF THE ROYAL CASTLE

The castle courtyard is one of the finest examples of Italian renaissance architecture in Poland. Built in such a grand style the royal castle on Wawel was intended to reflect the magnificence of Sigismund the Elder and the extent of the power of the Jagiellonian dynasty, which at the beginning of the 16th century extended over Poland, Lithuania, Bohemia and Hungary, covering an area from the Baltic to the Adriatic, from the mouth of the Elbe to the Dneiper.

The portico and the first two orders of arcading surrounding the courtyard form covered walks which on the ground and first floor are protected by renaissance arches, while on the top storey protection from the damp climate is provided by a steeply sloping roof with gutters, supported by slender columns. Fragments of 16th-century frescoes are still visible on the walls. Along the south side there is a wall, also decorated with arches and with trompe l'œil windows in which we see the sky and the tops of the trees growing on the ulica Bernardyńska side of the hill. There have been numerous excavations in the courtyard area, and the west end of a romanesque complex has been discovered. Among the finds was the crypt of St Gereon, whose name is linked with the legend of a mysterious stone, which according to the Hindus is the seventh chakra of the Earth. Scholars have found accounts of Indian travellers who came to the courtyard in Cracow to perform secret contemplations. The stone, whose exact whereabouts has never been discovered, is believed to be the source of extraordinary energy endowing men with superhuman powers of strength and endurance.

Those denying the stone's existence interpret the story as one of many signs of the increasingly widespread ideas of the New Age. Those who give it credence remember that the first visitors came here from the East in the 1930s and are not in the least bit worried by the opinion that the legend is the outcome of post-modern interest in oriental exoticism.

Flowers in the Wikarówka
window (the Vicar's House).

The loggias in the north
wing of the castle.

Windows in the east wing of
the Castle and fragments of
the original fresco decoration.

The staircase on the
ground floor of the castle.

SETTLEMENTS ON WAWEL

It is more than 5,000 years since the earliest permanent
settlements appeared on Wawel. In the Palaeolithic period it was first occupied by nomads who were replaced by small peasant communities in the Neolithic
period. In the bronze and iron ages there were further
settlements. Over the centuries a small fortified town
grew up on the hill with the castle of the ruler, later the
king, at its centre. In the "city of Wawel", of which
few traces remain, the king's servants had their
dwellings. In the 19th century a barracks and military
hospital were also built on the hill.

In recent years efforts have been concentrated on the
creation of the Wawel museum and on preserving the
symbolic power of the ancient site, but nevertheless
the settlement's abiding link with common man has
not been forgotten.

Signs of this human element can be seen today in the
pots of flowers decorating the windows of the
"Wikarówka" (Vicar's house) where the Cathedral
priests live. The employees of the Wawel museums
live in the houses to the north-west of the hill.

Panoramic view of Wawel from the Vistula.

THE PANORAMA OF WAWEL
FROM THE VISTULA

The panorama of Wawel to be enjoyed from the opposite bank of the Vistula has changed considerably over the centuries. For many years the dominant features were the three towers of the Cathedral: the Sigismund Tower (*Wieża Zygmuntowska*), the Clock Tower (*Wieża Zegarowa*) and the Tower of the Silver Bells (*Wieża Srebrnych Dzwonów*). The row of houses from various periods to the right of the Cathedral includes the house of the College of Cantor Chaplains, the house of the Mansionaries, and the ex-Seminary. The oldest and

closest to the Cathedral was built during the reign of Casimir the Great and was originally intended for the king. It was later used as a granary before passing, under Sigismund the Elder, to the College of Cantor Chaplains, those members of the choir in the service of the royal chapel. The College was composed of the master, ten cantor priests and an altar-boy, and it gave uninterrupted service from 1540 to 1872. The 15th-century building beside the Chaplains' house was the home of the Cathedral Mansionaries from the 18th century. The neighbouring Seminary is housed in three buildings, originally built in the 15th century but consistently renovated and its present appearance is the result of 18th-

On the following pages: the Cathedral and the ▶
"dom rorantystów" (house of the cantor priests).
The monument to Tadeusz Kościuszko with the
Sigismund Tower in the background.

century restoration. The Wawel ecclesiastical institute
was active from 1682 to 1801, when it was closed by the
Austrians. At the beginning of this century the Cathedral
Museum (founded 1906) was set up in the old Seminary
buildings together with the Ethnographic Museum
(founded in 1913, closed by the Germans in 1939, and re-
opened after the war in the Kazimierz Town Hall).
The next stretch of the panorama includes the adminis-
trative headquarters of the State Art Collection, replac-
ing the characteristic block, with three wings, of the
Austrian military hospital which stood there in the last
century. Further on, at the base of the square Thieves'
Tower, below the city walls, is the Dragon's Opening.

The oldest account of the Wawel dragon legend is in
the Polish Chronicles (*Chronika Polonorum*) compiled
by Vincent Kadłubek on the orders of Duke Casimir
the Just (1138-94). In it we learn of a terrible dragon
who ate cows and men, frightening the inhabitants of
Cracow. One day Prince Grakch, whom the locals
came to call Krak (and hence the city's name), arrived
from Carinthia and on being proclaimed king decided
to kill the monstrous dragon. Grakch's sons threw a
cow stuffed with sulphur inside the beast's cave: he ate
it and died. (In the socialist-realist version the hero of
the tale was a poor cobbler who threw the dragon a
ram similarly stuffed.)

Wawel: the road leading to the north entrance.

The Clock Tower.

The Wawel panorama ends on the left with another old Austrian military hospital and the Sandomierz Tower, where members of the nobility from the eponymous region were held prisoner. The oldest document relating to the tower is dated 1467 when six Cracowian citizens found guilty of the murder of the powerful lord, Jedrzej Teczynski, were executed. That crime, celebrated in contemporary ballads, gave rise to the most famous court-case in 15th-century Poland.

THE ROAD TO WAWEL

The road leading from the Old City to Wawel was for many centuries the only link between the low-land and the top of the hill (the other access from the south side was built in the 19th century). The old road leads along the north wing of the Castle and ascends parallel to the left side of the Cathedral with its two towers, the Sigismund Tower and the Clock Tower which dominate the landscape on this side of the hill. The Sigismund Tower takes its name from King Sigismund the Elder, as does its enormous bell (the entrance to the tower is in the Cathedral sacristy). The bell was founded in 1520 and exemplifies Polish bell-founding at its greatest. It is rung on rare occasions, giving rise to the idiom *od wielkiego dzwonu* ("at the sound of the great bell" i.e. "very rarely"). The "Zygmunt", 260 cm in diameter and 195 cm high, weighs about 11 tons (the clapper alone weighs 300 kgs) and eight or ten men are needed to ring it. It was founded by Jan Behem with bronze from canons taken in Walachia.

The road which rises so steeply to the monumental buildings on the summit is supported by a wall covered in plaques. These commemorate all those who helped to restore Wawel after the years of damage suffered under the Austrian occupation. Through the first gate stands the equestrian statue to Tadeusz Kościuszko, the Polish national hero. His peasant costume, under which we can discern his tunic, breast-plate and throat-piece, symbolises the massive peasant uprising in defence of their country (in 1794 their role in the uprising was certainly far from passive). The statue is the work of the architect and sculptor Leonard Marconi (1835-99), professor at the Leopoli Polytechnic. It was originally placed in the courtyard

The King's Bedroom.

The Chapel.

of the Central Fire-station, but professor Adolf Szyszko-Bohusz, director of the Wawel restoration, found it a more suitable site on the Wladyslaw IV bastion. In 1939 the monument was damaged by the Nazis. Restored and returned to Cracow after the war by the city of Dresden, it was replaced on the bastion in 1960. The Clock Tower, with a gothic base but completed in the baroque style by Kacper Bażanka, retains fragments of stone from the 12th-century romanesque cathedral. The four statues on the top of the tower are of St Casimir, patron saint of Lithuania, St Wenceslas, the patron of the Cathedral, St Stanisław, who is buried in the Cathedral, and St Adalbert, the patron saint of Poland.

THE ROYAL APARTMENTS

The idea of creating a museum in the Royal Apartments was first mooted in the second half of the 19th century, but was impossible to realise at that stage as the castle was being used as a barracks by the occupying Austrian forces. It took several decades to

The Senators' Chamber: detail.

collect sufficient funds to ransom the castle from the enemy and it was only after the Austrian retreat that the long needed restoration work could begin.

The castle interior had been almost ruined with the loss of many of the fine decorative details in both wood and stone. It was impossible to see the original fresco work. Scarcely anything survived of the decoration in the King's apartments: even the fine majolica stoves had been lost. The art collection was dispersed, some of it having been taken abroad. The first task was to salvage any surviving elements from the original structure and to demolish the alterations made by the Austrians to adapt the interior to a barracks. When the plaster was removed from the walls faded frescoes were revealed. All that remained of the coffered wooden ceilings were some of the rosette decoration and some of the carving on the beams. Thirty carved

heads, portraits of 16th-century figures, were saved from the Throne Room. There were enough surviving fragments to reconstruct the window surrounds in *pietra serena*. The *kurdybany* (painted and embossed leather used as wall hangings) was brought back from the castle of August III at Mortizburg, while seven 18th-century majolica stoves were brought from the castle at Wisniowiec in Wolinia to replace the original renaissance ones. The generosity of individual donations was of enormous help in the restoration work and has continued to be a major factor in enriching the Wawel art collections. The primary concern of those engaged on the restoration was to recapture the original appearance of the rooms, making use of 16th-century and later descriptions, court accounts and the registration of payment for work and materials, together with those surviving pieces whose authenticity could be guaranteed.

THE KING'S TAPESTRIES

The rich collection of tapestries decorating the castle walls are the finest examples of renaissance art in Poland. The survival of these remarkable works provides the museum interiors with an impressive reminder of the castle's original splendour. The earliest examples in the collection were sixteen tapestries in the Gobelin style commissioned by Sigismund I from the Antwerp workshop in 1526. Seven years later the king commissioned a further ninety-two tapestries. Sigismund's son Sigismund Augustus (1548-72) inherited his father's enthusiasm for tapestries and had several hundred of them delivered to Cracow from the Brussels workshop. The collection of Sigismund Augustus II included some 350 or perhaps 365 tapestries, as some sources say the number equalled the days in the year, which were hung on the castle walls according to contemporary taste. The widespread use of tapestries in interior decoration at the time is reflected in the works of Shakespeare. Falstaff in the *Merry Wives of Windsor*, and Polonius in *Hamlet*, hide behind such hangings. With the extinction of the Jagiellonian dynasty the tapestries became the property of the Republic and were kept in the Royal Treasury. They played a crucial role in the period of the Swedish invasions (1655-57), for after being hidden from the predatory soldiers of Karl Gustavus and hidden in the mountains they were deposited in Danzig in return for the necessary funds for John Casimir to conduct the war of liberation. Redeemed by Poland in 1724 they were first kept in a Warsaw convent and later in the Krasiński Palace, where they remained until the fall of the Polish monarchy. Catherine II of Russia had the tapestries taken out of Poland and they remained in the Russian collections during all the years of foreign domination. They were finally restored to Poland in 1921 after peace was concluded with Russia at Riga. The collection had become severely depleted over the years with castle fires and other vicissitudes. Of Sigismund Augustus's 365 tapestries only 136 returned to the castle rooms. Their travels were not at an end however for

The Senators' Chamber

One of the tapestries in the series showing
Scenes from the life of Noah.

Above: tapestry, detail.

Below left:
tapestry with monogram of Sigismund Augustus.
Below right:
one of the tapestries in the series showing
Scenes from the life of Noah.

in September 1939 all the Wawel treasures were removed to safety, first to Romania and then in 1940 to Canada. They were returned to Poland in 1961 and the collection now includes 140 pieces. Its extraordinary value is enhanced by two factors: first, the tapestries are hung in the rooms for which they were originally intended; secondly, they are one of the few examples of such a collection commissioned by a single king. The bulk of the collection was commissioned in the 1560s and 1570s, a relatively short period of time, from a famous factory, Brussels. They are woven in wool and silk thread enriched with gold and silver. The compositions are adapted from cartoons by Michiel Coxcie (1499-1592), a famous Flemish mannerist who worked in Rome, where he became a member of the Academy of San Luca, and in Brussels where he was nick-named the "Flemish Raphael". His works, with their obvious debt to the Italian Renaissance, are remarkable for their

fine compositions. The flora and fauna motifs and the grotesques were taken from cartoons by artists in the circle of Pieter Coecke van Aelst and of Cornelis Floris and of Cornelis Bos. The Wawel tapestries were made in a variety of shapes and sizes suited to their original positioning, in which many of them are now to be found. In the Throne Room, also called "the Ambassadors' Room" or "Under the Heads" (the coffered ceiling is decorated with wooden heads, carved by Sebastian Tauerbach and Jan Snycerz) are the wonderful tapestries in the series of *The Stories of Adam and Eve*, that decorated the room at the time of Sigismund Augustus. The Senators' Room also houses the series of *Scenes from the life of Noah* in their original order, as they appeared on the day of the wedding between Sigismund Augustus and the Archduchess Catherine in 1553, and as they are described in contemporary chronicles.

The Merlini Room.

THE MERLINI ROOM

In the architectural complex of Wawel the finest buildings belong to the gothic, renaissance and baroque periods and there are relatively few examples of the neo-classical style, which became evident in Polish architecture with the accession to the throne in 1764 of Stanisław Augustus Poniatowski, the last king of Poland. It is to him we owe the neo-classical conception of the Merlini Room. When Stanisław Augustus elected to receive the royal insignia in Warsaw he broke with tradition. His decision was based on the deplorable condition of the Wawel Castle at the time, hardly suited to the happy inauguration of a new reign. Immediately after his coronation the king sent the court architect Domenico Merlini (1730-97) to Cracow: Between 1786 and 1787 he worked on the renovation of the old Hall of the Silver Mirrors, creating the Silver Room which differs from all the other castle interiors in its cold interpretation of classical form. The room has 18th-century furniture from the Bishop's Palace in Kielce. The paintings by Marcello Baciarelli, court-painter to Stanisław Augustus, are in perfect harmony with the architectural setting. The visit by the last Polish king to Wawel, the occasion for all the renovations, proved to be his last. The main reason for the visit was a penitential pilgrimage to the tomb of St Stanisław, undertaken by every Polish monarch before his coronation in order to obtain the protection of the Saint, who had been killed and dishonoured by King Boleslaw the Bold. In the case of the only king to share the Saint's name his prayers appeared ineffective. After the failure of the reforms King Stanisław had promised and after the third Partition of Poland the king abdicated and died a few years later in exile in Russia.

THE PAINTINGS IN THE WAWEL COLLECTION

The paintings in the State Art Collection at Wawel include works by Polish artists and from other European schools, either donated to or purchased by the Museum. The most valuable gifts and acquisitions are those relating to the history of the castle or those belonging to a period in perfect harmony with the other works displayed. The first group includes the portraits of sovereigns and Polish magnates painted by Crakowian artists and commissioned by the court. The second group includes baroque paintings, mostly Flemish and Dutch, which decorate the rooms in the north wing of the castle as well as Italian works of the 15th and 16th centuries in the renaissance rooms in the east wing. One of these is the 15th-century tondo of the Florentine school showing the Christ Child being given to the Madonna and St Joseph by the Angel Gabriel. The painting hangs in the Tournament Room.

A tondo, Florentine school, 15th century.

◀ Aerial view of Wawel Cathedral

View of the south side of Wawel Cathedral.

THE CATHEDRAL OF WAWEL

The first cathedral was built on Wawel in circa 1020 when, as a result of negotiations at Gniezo, the Emperor Otto III gave his consent to King Boleslaw the Intrepid to institute the Polish ecclesiastical hierarchy. All that remains of the first cathedral is the crypt dedicated to St Gereon which lies at the same level as the cellars in the west wing of the castle. All that survives of the second, romanesque building, is the St Leonard crypt, the lower part of the Tower with the Silver Bells, and the base of the Clock Tower. The gothic cathedral we see today is therefore the third ecclesiastical building erected on Wawel. Work began on the present construction in 1320 and it was consecrated in 1364. Over the centuries the Cathedral has been enlarged, new chapels have been added and the building has been made higher. Between 1895 and 1910 the last major reconstruction was carried out. From the middle of the 12th century the Cathedral was the centre of the cult of St Stanisław. From 1320 onwards all the Polish monarchs were crowned in the Cathedral with the exception of the last Stanisław Augustus Poniatowski, and many of them were also buried here. As well as providing the resting place for kings, the great Polish poets Adam Mickiewicz and Juliusz Słowacki and national heroes such as Tadeusz Kosćiuszko, Count Józef Poniatowski and Józef Piłsudski are also buried here. "This basilica is so closely associated with the history of the Polish Nation, with the best and worst moments of our monarchy, that if no written history of Poland were to survive, the walls and marble of this temple would narrate it all" was how the 18th-century bishop of Cracow, Józef Olechowschi, spoke of his cathedral.

The Tower of the Silver Bells and the Royal chapels.

On the following pages: the lantern with a cross above the dome of the King Sigismund Chapel. The south side of the Cathedral at dusk.

View of Wawel Cathedral from the village of Wawel.

THE SOUTH FAÇADE OF THE CATHEDRAL

The south façade of the Cathedral is interesting for the variety of architectural styles and elements it incorporates, from the romanesque to modern additions (the baldachin above the entrance to the crypt was designed by Adolf Szyszko-Bohusz in 1937). Projecting from the main gothic structure are two chapels, remarkable for their similarity: the renaissance *Kaplica Zygmuntowska* (King Sigismund Chapel), covered with a gilt dome, and the baroque *Kaplica Wazów* (Vasa Chapel), a hundred years later than the first but with an identical ground plan. They were both built as funerary chapels, and members of Poland's two ruling dynasties during the "golden century" were buried there. In the *Kaplica Zygmuntowska*, begun by Sigismund I, lie the tombs of the last two members of the Jagiellonian dynasty. The spherical vault and the plates covering the dome are coated with gold leaf of enormous value; miraculously

PLAN OF THE CATHEDRAL

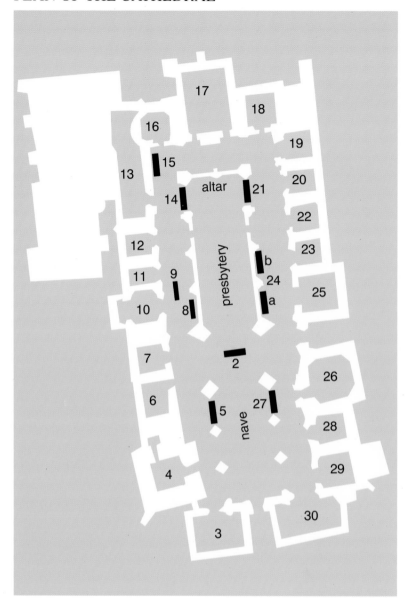

LEGENDA

1. Door decorated in iron, bearing the initials of Casimir the Great
2. Mausoleum of St Stanisław
3. Chapel of the Holy Cross
4. Czartoryski Chapel, entrance to the crypt with the tombs of the Kings
5. Funerary monument to Władysław Warneńczyk
6. St Nicholas Chapel
7. Bishop Maciejowski Chapel
8. Silver plaque depicting John III Sobieski before Vienna
9. Mickiewicz and Słowacki crypt
10. Lipski Chapel
11. Skotnicki Chapel
12. Bishop Zebrzydowski Chapel
13. Sacristy - corridor leading to the Sigismund Tower
14. Funerary monument to Władysław the Short
15. Altar to the Crucified Christ (the black gothic Crucifix)
16. Bishop Gamrat Chapel
17. Lady Chapel with the funerary monument to Stefan Batory
18. Bishop Tomicki Chapel
19. Bishop Załuski Chapel
20. Jan Olbracht Chapel
21. Funerary monument to Casimir the Great
22. Bishop Zadzik Chapel
23. Bishop Konarski Chapel
24.a\b Royal insignia of Queen Jadwiga and her funerary monument
25. Sigismund Chapel
26. Vasa Chapel
27. Funerary monument to Władysław Jagiello
28. Szafraniec Chapel
29. Potocki Chapel
30. Holy Cross Chapel

A view of the nave of the Cathedral.

and despite Cracow's many insurgencies the treasure of the cupola has remained untouched. The *Kaplica Wazow* was planned in 1598 by King Sigismund Vasa who, like his predecessor, was profoundly affected by the death of his wife. Work was barely begun on the chapel during the reign of their son John Casimir. While the two chapels are remarkably similar from the outside they differ greatly on the inside.

INSIDE THE CATHEDRAL: THE ST STANISŁAW MAUSOLEUM

The black stone portal with wooden doors covered in metal bearing one of the great coats of arms of Cracow, the initial K of King Casimir the Great surmounted by a crown, leads into the Cathedral. In the great nave we are immediately confronted with the St

Tapestries and the St Stanisław Mausoleum -
view from the Cathedral Choir.

The St Stanisław Mausoleum.

St Cross Chapel: funerary monument to ▶
Bishop Kajetan Sołtyk.

Stanisław Mausoleum, a monument of enormous religious significance and of considerable artistic interest.
The silver sarcophagus containing the remains of the
saint is a masterpiece of 17th-century goldsmiths'
work. It was made in 1670 in Danzig in the workshop
of Piotr van der Renner, and is decorated with twelve
reliefs depicting scenes from the Saint's life together
with the miracles attributed to him after his death. The
black marble baldachin above the sarcophagus is an
earlier work by Giovanni Trevano (1626-30). St
Stanisław of Szczepanowo was bishop of Cracow from
about 1030 until his death in 1079, and the legend of
his life and death is related in the chronicles of
Vincent Kadłubek, although the events he recalls in
1200 are not fully confirmed by other historical evidence. What is certain is that the dramatic conflict between the Bishop Stanisław and King Bolesław II the
Bold was of a political nature and ended in the
Bishop's death by quartering. The legend attributes re-
sponsibility for his death directly to the king, and
states that Bolesław himself gave the order "to have
him quartered" but that afterwards the saint's body
was miraculously reunited. The saint's reunification
was interpreted as a prophetic sign of the imminent reunification of the Polish kingdom which was then divided into small feudal duchies. The spread of the cult
of the Bishop-Martyr led to his canonisation in 1253
and from that time his tomb has been a centre of pilgrimage. From 1320, the year in which the kingdom
was restored, every new Polish monarch has processed
to the church of *Na Skalce*, where the Bishop was murdered, in expiation for Bolesław's sin. The legend of
St Stanisław also states that any bearing his name
would not remain on the Polish throne. In the 18th
century, despite this warning, Stanisław Dąbski was
nominated bishop of Cracow but he died before his in-
vestiture. Also two newly crowned kings of Poland,
Stanisław Leszczyński and Stanisław Augustus
Poniatowski, were forced to abdicate.

THE TOMBS OF THE KINGS

The rich decoration of the Cathedral and the numerous monuments and works of artistic interest contained in it, despite the extraordinary stylistic variety, create an overall impression of harmony which has been nurtured over the years. A careful study of all these works of historical interest requires far more time than the survey afforded it by most visitors to the Cathedral. For all its great interest, this Sanctuary to the memory of the Nation has never been merely a museum, and its life continues to be that of a place of worship, it has always been.

The sculptural effigies on the tombs of the Polish kings and bishops are the most important group of monuments inside the Cathedral. They were carved by both Polish and foreign sculptors working in Poland, including Weit Stoss, Bartolomeo Berrecci, Jan Michałowicz of Urdędowo, Santi Gucci and Antoni Madeyski. Madeyski (1869-1939) was responsible for two of the funerary monuments: those of Wladyslaw III and of Queen Jadwiga. The tomb of King

Wawel Cathedral: one of the stained-glass windows.

The baroque interior of the Vasa Chapel.

The tomb of Blessed Queen Jadwiga, sculpted by
Antoni Madeyski.

Władysław is empty. The body of the young king, killed in the battle of Varna (1444) while leading a daring attack against the Janissaries, was never recovered. The remains of Queen Jadwiga were placed in her tomb in 1949. The daughter of Louis d'Anjou, King of Hungary, and granddaughter of Władysław the Short, she succeeded to the Polish throne at the age of ten. She was renowned for her saintliness during her lifetime, and after her death at the end of the 14th century her cult spread. The places she was known to have visited and everything connected with her life (including the black gothic Crucifix in the north aisle before which she frequently prayed) became objects of veneration. The apparent lack of interest on the part of the Catholic Church in her beatification led to the progressive weakening of her cult. Work on part of the Cathedral presbytery meant that her burial place was also forgotten. It was rediscovered in 1887 and in 1949 was opened and her remains were moved to the sepulchre of white Carrara marble carved by Madeyski. This work with its cold poetry and classical linearity is decorated with a frieze of eagles reflecting more modernist taste. Jadwiga's mortal remains were moved again in 1987 in preparation for her beatification, a ceremony presided over by Pope John Paul II.

In the past there was not the concern that exists today for the preservation of works of historical interest, a

91

Wawel Cathedral: funerary Chapel of King Stefan Batory with the painting of the *Częstochowa Madonna*.

The King Sigismund Chapel: tombs of ▶ the last Jagiellonian kings.

negligence reflected in the histories of the presbytery and the chapels off the aisles. They were built in the middle ages but repeatedly rebuilt and sometimes demolished to make room for the construction of more modern chapels. In the years 1387-90 the Chapel to the Virgin was built, originally fulfilling the role of a minor choir. At the end of the 16th century Anna Jagiello had the chapel transformed into the funerary chapel for Stefan Batory and the marble monument to the king by the Florentine Santi Gucci was placed there. Gucci worked in Cracow for many years in the Italian mannerist style. The figure of the king, sculpted in low-relief, does not appear to be the likeness of a dead man but rather the portrait of a sleeping one with a soft smile on his lips and making a natural gesture with his hand. The details in black marble were added in 1648 by the Vasa who showed particular enthusiasm for this material.

THE KING SIGISMUND CHAPEL
(Kaplica Zygmuntowska)

Kaplica Zygmuntowska differs from all the other chapels in the Cathedral for the purity of its style, never having undergone restoration. It was built by Bartolomeo Berrecci from Pontassieve near Florence, who was summoned to Cracow by Sigismund I. Art historians are astounded by the fact that Berrecci, hardly recognised at home, succeeded in Cracow in creating such a sublime work which despite being a funerary chapel conveys such a clarity of vision and sense of spiritual peace and well-being. The first drawings for the chapel were presented to the king in 1517, and in 1519 the foundations were laid. It took nine years to build and was completed in 1533. The colour scheme is limited to the gold of the inscriptions, the white of the walls and the red marble of the

The King Sigismund Chapel: tomb of Queen Anne Jagiello.

monuments to Sigismund I and his children Sigismund Augustus and Anna Jagiello. The square plan covered by a dome is in the pure Renaissance style. To the left of the entrance Berrecci placed an altar made in Nuremberg after a design by Hans Dürer. The statues in the side niches are of St Peter and St Paul, St Wenceslas, the first patron saint of Cracow, St Florian, St John the Baptist and St Sigismund, the patron saint of the king who commissioned the chapel. In the roundels above are busts of the four Evangelists together with two biblical kings: Solomon, depicted in the likeness of Sigismund I, and David, portrayed as Seweryn Boner, administrator of the royal domains and supervisor of the construction of the chapel. The funerary slab to Anna Jagiello, placed there in 1596, was carved while the queen was still alive. The cost of building the chapel, excluding the gilding of the cupola, amounted to 25,727 florins, the equivalent of 67.5 kgs of solid gold.

The Church of St Bernardino: baroque interior (1670-80).

CHURCH OF ST BERNARDINO
(Kościół św. Bernardyna)

Leaving Wawel by the south side we reach the Sandomierz Tower, in ulica Bernardyńska, where the church dedicated to St Bernardino of Siena also stands, darkened over the years and covered with ivy. The baroque church was built between 1670 and 1680 to replace the gothic structure of some 200 years earlier and destroyed by the Swedes in 1655. The beautiful wide façade of the church is flanked by two low octagonal towers with square bases, surmounted by lanterns. The façade is divided into three unequal sections by architraves providing contrast to the vertical pilasters symmetrically arranged around the niches filled with statues. The church was designed by Krzysztof Mieroszewski (1600-76), one of the most talented Polish architects of the 17th century. Until 1648 he was secretary to Władysław IV Vasa. He was trained as a military engineer and specialised in the construction of fortresses; the church of St Bernardino is one of his last works, unfinished at the time of his death. The sumptuous baroque interior is still intact. The painting of the Virgin of Sokal, crowned in 1724, is in the Sanctuary of the Virgin. In the north chapel there is a sculpture of *St Anne with the Virgin and Child* attributed to Weit Stoss. The splendid baroque interior, inspiring visitors to contemplation, also serves as the setting for concerts of early music.

OKÓŁ

ULICA KANONICZA

Leaving Wawel on foot in the direction of Rynek Główny we can choose either the old royal route, that is ulica Grodzka, or the longer, much more picturesque route along the ulica Kanonicza. The ulica Kanonica runs from the lively ulica Podzamcze where we find the 600-year-old house of Długosz. This originally housed the Jagiellonian baths but was later purchased by Jan di Niedzisko. Niedzisko, a survivor of the Grunwald campaign, was the father of a dozen children who all bore their father's Christian name of Jan. One of these, Jan Długosz (known as Longinus, 1415-80), was the author of the monumental *Historia Polonica*. He was born in this house and it was here he wrote his twelve-volume history in clear Latin in the style of Livy. Stanisław Wyspiański (1869-1907), the most Cracowian of all Polish artists, also lived here as a child. He is commemorated in the stone plaque with words taken from his poetry, and mention is also made of the workshop belonging to his father, the sculptor Fraciszek Wyspiański.

Ulica Kanonicza-probably the most characteristic street in the Old City.

Aerial view of *Plac Wita Stwosza* (Weit Stoss Square), formerly the market in the Okół district.

The Church of St Andrew - the largest romanesque church in Cracow.

THE CENTRE OF OKÓŁ

Ulica Grodza, which runs parallel to ulica Kanonicza is the direct and most frequented route from Rynek Główny to Wawel. The street has many buildings of historic interest such as no. 43, the *Collegium Juridicum*, part of the University since 1403, no. 38, where Weit Stoss had his workshop, and the gothic church of St Giles, probably built on the foundations of an earlier romanesque church. The most characteristic stretch of ulica Grodzka runs through plac Wita Stwosza, after which it joins ulica Kanonicza. On the east side of the square are two churches in contrasting styles: the baroque church of St Peter and St Paul and the romanesque church of St Andrew. Before the *locatio civitatis* of Cracow this square was the centre of the first community to develop around Wawel which had escaped the destruction caused by the Tartar invasion of 1241. The densely populated area of Okół was surrounded by a rampart. The word Okół in fact denotes a walled area ('*okolony*'). Archaeological excavations testify to the existence of settlements here ever since the 7th century.

The centre of the Okół district, the first suburb in Cracow.

THE CHURCH OF ST ANDREW
(Kościół św. Andrzeja)

Built on a basilican plan with blocks of white limestone, the church of St Andrew has a nave with side aisles and a transept, with the main entrance on the north side. The west façade, looking onto ulica Grodzka, is flanked by two towers with square bases which become octagonal at the height of the roof of the nave. The lanterns on top of the towers, built in 1639, are in perfect harmony with the romanesque building and St Andrew's, dating from the second half of the 11th century, is the best preserved of the romanesque churches in Cracow. The church was built by Duke Włodzisław Herman, who ruled from 1079 to 1102; he founded many churches dedicated to St Giles as votive offerings for the birth of his son Bolesław. Their dedication to St Giles was in recognition of the prayers of l'abbaye de Saint-Gilles in Provence, petitioned by the Duke, for the birth of a son and heir. The present dedication to St Andrew is rare among the churches founded by Włodzisław. The Latin chronicles of the Anonymous Gaul (Gallus Anonimus) quote from a letter, accompanied by rich gifts and sent by the Duke to the abbot of Saint-Gilles: "We, Włodzisław, Duke of Poland by the grace of God, and Judith our lawful consort, send our humble respects to the venerable abbot of Saint-Gilles and to all the monks, and acknowledging how superior St Gilles is to all others in devotion and in his willingness to assist the faithful with the power conferred on him from above, we are desirous to offer him our obsequious gifts *in voto* for the long desired birth of an heir and we humbly beseech your prayers for that intention".

The austere romanesque structure is in sharp contrast to its rich baroque interior. In 1320 it became the property of an order of Carmelite nuns whose convent stands beside the church. It was given to them by Wladyslaw I the Short and tradition has it that his crown was made from the gold found between the limestone blocks of the church walls, hidden there by the inhabitants of Okoł during the Tartar invasions.

The Church of St Peter and St Paul.

THE CHURCH OF ST PETER AND ST PAUL
(Kościół św. św. Piotra i Pawła)

The church of St Peter and St Paul is an enormous baroque edifice built at the beginning of the 17th century and strongly influenced by Italian baroque architecture, especially by the churches of the Gesù and of Sant' Andrea della Valle in Rome. It was the first baroque church in Cracow, built in response to the arrival of the Jesuits in Poland in 1583. The Society of Jesus was first based at the church of St Barbara, but at the end of the 16th century the new church was begun. This had to be demolished shortly after construction began because of severe miscalculations. After further vicissitudes the new commission was given to Giovan Battista Trevano, who also built the St Stanisław mausoleum in the Cathedral on Wawel. Above the crossing is a large dome, recently restored, decorated by Giovan Battista Falconi, the first Baroque sculptor to work in Cracow. He was also responsible for the stucco decoration in the apse depicting the *Death of St Peter and St Paul*. The dome was completed in 1619

The Church of St Peter and St Paul: the façade overlooking ulica Grodza.

The Church of St Peter and St Paul: detail of the façade. ▶

and its decoration in 1633. The interior has a single nave flanked by intercommunicating chapels. The Jesuit writer, Piotr Skarga (1536-1612), is buried in the crypt below the presbytery. He was the author of the *Sermons to the Diet*, a political tract divided into eight sermons setting forth his ideas regarding the State and Government. At the time of the Polish *Respublica*'s greatest military and territorial power his sermons were not favourably received and he was criticised for fomenting trouble and predicting future disaster and the ruin of the State. The Romantics, especially Mickiewicz in the course of his studies at the Collège de France, recognised him as a prophetic voice and quoted the following extracts from the ser-

mons written at the beginning of the 17th century: "All this peace and all this idleness which you hold so dear will be transformed into affliction and misery. The cruelty imposed on your subjects for your own profit will be turned against you. You will find yourselves in the cruel hands of your enemies who will oppress you more than you have oppressed your people, and will burden you with a heavy yoke and give you no relief either by day or by night". Jan Matejko also contributed to the fame of Skarga in his celebrated painting *The sermons of Skarga* showing the Jesuit in the presence of the thoughtful King Sigismund III, uttering dire predictions for the future of the State.

The Church of St Peter and St Paul: railings with the statues of the twelve Apostles.

THE TWELVE APOSTLES

The small square in front of the church of St Peter and St Paul is enclosed by wrought-iron railings including twelve pedestals supporting baroque statues in white stone of the twelve Apostles. They are the work of Daniel (or perhaps of David) Hell and of Ferdinand Kilcz, and were carved around 1723. The soft stone from which they are sculpted has suffered considerably over the years from erosion and acid rain. The statues,

having lost noses and with fingers corroded, were moved under a special shelter but this hardly improved the situation. The statues now in the square are copies of the originals made by Kazimierz Jeczmyk. The restoration of the originals took some twenty years. Acid rain was the result of the pollution from the iron and steel industries near Cracow, from the use of coal-fired heating in the Old City, as well as from insufficient air movement in the valley of the Vistula aggravated by urban planning after the war in the areas to the east of the city.

◄The Church of St Francis of Assisi and the monument to Professor Józef Dietl.

The neo-gothic tympanum above the gothic stone door to the Dominican Church.

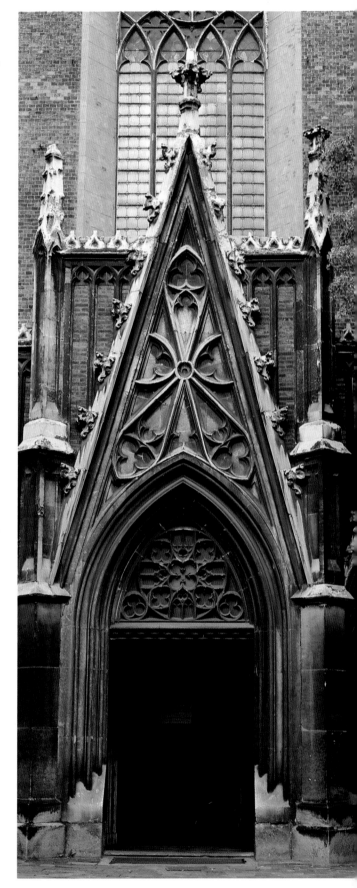

THE OLDEST GOTHIC CHURCHES IN CRACOW

There are two adjacent squares off ulica Grodza : Plac Wszystkich Swiętych (All Saints square), with the **church of St Francis**, and Plac Dominikański (the square of the Dominicans) with the **Dominican church**. These two churches are among the oldest monuments in Cracow. The church and convent of the Franciscans were built in 1236, supposedly by the Silesian Duke Henry II the Pious for the Franciscans, newly arrived from Prague. Finished in 1269 the church was the scene of many dramatic events including the baptism of the Lithuanian Duke Jagiello (Jagiello then took the name of Władysław) in 1296, and the murder in his sacristy of Jędrzej Tęczyński by a mob of merchants in 1461. Fire destroyed the original gothic decoration but the present interior which dates from the end of the 19th century includes some remarkable Liberty-style frescoes on the walls of the transept and presbytery by Stanisław Wyspiański, who also made the beautiful stained glass windows in the apse with the Blessed Salome, St Francis and the monumental figure of God the Father. The Stations of the Cross are the work of Józef Mehoffer.

In Plac Wszystkich Swietych there stands a monument to Professor Józef Dietl, a doctor, Rector of the Jagiellonian University, Mayor of the city 1866-74, and celebrated for his research of the Carpazi thermal waters. The statue is the work of Xawery Dunikowski (1875-1964).

On the other side of the street is the fine Dominican church and convent: the oldest buildings in Cracow to be made of brick and also the first examples of the gothic style in the city. Built after 1223, it preserves remains of an earlier stone romanesque construction. The building of the church, on the basilican plan, with

The Church of Corpus Domini in Kazimierz,
founded by Casimir the Great.

a nave flanked by single side aisles with many chapels, was finished about 1300, but in the course of the first century after its completion it suffered various alterations terminating in the construction of the magnificent portal in 1400. In the presbytery there is a tomb slab to Filip Kallimach (Callimacus), cast in bronze in Nuremberg in the workshop of Peter Vischer on the design of Weit Stoss. Callimacus (Filippo Buonaccorsi of San Gimignano) was tutor to the children of Casimir Jagiello and the foremost humanist poet at the court of Cracow. His tomb bears the oldest Polish epitaph to a layman who was not of royal family. In the north aisle a small stairway leads to the chapel of St Hyacinth built after 1545 on a renaissance plan and later enriched with baroque decoration. The Myszkowski chapel of 1614 opens off the south aisle and is one of the "Sarmatian" chapels of the golden century, the first being the King Sigismund chapel and the last the Vasa chapel. The neo-gothic portal built in 1850 harmonises perfectly with the church's gothic façade.

KAZIMIERZ

THE CHURCH OF CORPUS DOMINI IN KAZIMIERZ
(Kościół Bożego Ciała na Kazimierzu)

In the 14th century an independent community developed on the other side of the Vistula, which in 1335 was awarded *locatio civitatis* by King Casimir the Great. This meant that it gained recognition as an independent city and was given the name Kazimierz. It re-

mained independent until 1796 when it became part of Cracow. In 1872 a tributary of the Vistula bordering the city to the north was filled in and a large avenue was planted, now become a road, the Planty Dietla. Several of the buildings in Kazimierz bear witness to its original independence: the ex-town-hall in plac Wolnica, the remains of the old city wall, churches, synagogues and even the name of the street leading to the Old City in Cracow, ulica Cracowska. Casimir III has always been celebrated as the great Polish restorer:

The monastery of Canons Regular beside the Church of Corpus Domini in Kazimierz.

The Church of Corpus Domini - the sumptuous ▶ baroque interior is in sharp contrast to the austere gothic architecture.

it is said that he found a Poland built of wood but left one made of stone. In fact during the forty years of his reign he built some fifty castles, founded many cities, twenty-seven of which were surrounded by city walls, and hundreds of villages. If we also consider all the churches and convents he had built the truth of the maxim appears far from exaggerated. One of his foundations was the church of Corpus Domini on the northeast corner of plac Wolnica. It has never suffered from fire, unlike so many churches in Cracow, and the gothic structure of the nave of the church is perfectly pre-

served. Construction began in 1340 and lasted more than 60 years, work being directed by the Czipser family, Cracowians of Hungarian origin. The main part of the building was probably finished in 1405 when Jan Czipser presented his accounts. In the second half of the 15th century the west façade was castellated on the gable, while its unusual bell-tower was built sometime later. The lower part of the interior has been decorated with sumptuous baroque taste but as the eye travels upwards we see the unaltered gothic purity of the original vaulting.

Aerial view of the Jewish City: the area around the old synagogue.

The old synagogue, now the Museum of the History of the City of Cracow.

JEWISH LIFE IN CRACOW

The first mention we have of Cracow is in reference to the punishment of a Jew, Ibrahin-Ibn Yacub, and ever since its earliest history the city has been closely associated with Jews. From the 10th century onwards caravans of Arab and Jewish merchants began to arrive in the city and it is assumed that the first Jewish communities settled at the foot of Wawel at this time, although some consider that the first colonies developed towards the end of the 11th century: historical sources refer to these colonies at the end of the 12th and the beginning of the 13th century. The reason for the growth of the Jewish community was twofold: Jews sought refuge from persecution in western Europe, particularly violent at the time of the Black Death (1349-50), and Poland encouraged urban colonisation especially under Casimir the Great. The first Jewish settlement grew up in the area around the present ulica św. Anny which was at that time ulica żydowska (The Jews' Street). Documents reveal that the present site of the *Collegium Maius* was a market square called the Jews' Market. Another small community soon developed into one of considerable size in Kazimierz. The same king who gave his name to that city settled it with Jewish refugees from Germany and France. In 1334 Casimir regularised their legal status in Poland. Throughout the reign of Casimir III the Great both Jewish communities continued to develop without hindrance, unusual in Europe at that time where ethnic-religious conflicts were rife. It is possible that an old word used by Jews for Poland, *Polin*, meaning "where peace is found", dates from this period. The increase in the population of Cracow and the growth of

The old synagogue: the *almēmōr* or *bīmah*, the place where the sentences of the *Kāhāl* court were pronounced.

The old synagogue: a beautiful doorway with its original decoration.

the German-speaking merchant class weakened the position of the Jews. While the Kazimierz community continued to prosper, the Jews of the old quarter around ulica Zydowska where moved to the north of the centre when the *Collegium Maius* was built. They did not remain there for long however because at the end of the 15th century King John Olbracht ordered them to leave Cracow after the outbreak of rioting. These Jews moved to Kazimierz, giving birth to the "Jewish City" which spread from plac Wolnica as far as its eastern and southern walls, so covering half of Cracow. The Kazimierz community's greatest prosperity coincided with the "golden century" of Poland. In the 16th century Poland, in contrast to the rest of Europe torn by religious discord, experienced a period of religious toleration and was defined as the "state without burning at the stake". The Jewish City enjoyed its own legal system and acted with considerable independence. Kazimierz became the capital of the *diaspora* welcoming refugees from the whole of central Europe. The old synagogue, built at the end of the 14th century at no. 24 ulica Szeroka, was rebuilt in the 16th century by Matteo Gucci in the same style as the synagogues of Ratisbon, Worms and Prague. During the last war the building was very badly damaged but has been reconstructed and now houses art and artefacts from the History Museum relating to Jewish culture in Cracow. The main room in the synagogue is where the faithful congregate to pray and it is here the 'bimah' or ornamental cage in wrought iron stands, from which the sentences of the 'kāhāl' are pronounced. It was here that Tadeusz Kośiuszko, leader of the 1794 insurrection, urged the Jews to fight in defence of their common homeland. At the outbreak of the second world war the Jewish community in Cracow amounted to 60,000 members, about 23% of the population. At the time of the closure of the ghetto by the Nazis, who had moved many families there from areas outside the city, its population was almost 70,000.

The Jewish cemetery: a wall built with fragments
of funerary steles.

The Remu'h cemetery: the renaissance tombs.

On 13 March 1943 the ghetto was destroyed: some of
the inhabitants were transported to the extermination
camp at Płaszów, while all the others were murdered
in the confines of the ghetto.

After the war when the Jewish cemetry at Remu'h was
excavated extremely old and precious tombs were discovered some 60 cm below the surface. They were
made of white sandstone from Pińczów and some
dated to the 16th century. They were placed here at the
beginning of the 18th century during the wars with the
North (1703-21), when the Swedish troops laid siege
to Cracow and Kazimierz. The earth proved the best
means of preserving these extraordinary tombs against
the ravages of time and the destruction of men.

The convent of the Norbertine nuns: the boatmen repulsed
the Tartar attack under these walls in 1281.

THE HISTORIC SUBURBS OF CRACOW

THE NORBERTINE CONVENT
AT ZWIERZYNIEC

One of the medieval suburbs of Cracow was
Zwierzyniec (incorporated into the city in 1910),
meaning 'hunting reserve' and it is first mentioned in
1224. Here, on the banks of the Vistula stands the
convent of the Norbertine nuns with their church ded-

icated to St Augustine. The founder of the convent
was the retired crusader Jaksa da Miechów. It was
begun in 1162 in the romanesque style but was destroyed by the Tartars in 1241. There is now no trace
of the gothic structure built to replace it, as both the
church and convent underwent massive reconstruction between the end of the 16th and the beginning of
the 17th century. In the 18th century they were fur-

ther provided with neo-classical interiors. The Norbertine convent is closely associated with the 'Zwierzyniec horse parade' or the 'Lajkonik', an historical celebration which has survived since the middle ages and is one of the most picturesque folk traditions in Cracow. Legend has it that at the time of the Tartar invasions members of the Boatmen's Guild attacked the Tartars who were besieging the convent and, having killed their Khan, made a victorious entry into Cracow dressed in the rich oriental robes of the invaders. Every June since then a colourful procession leaves the convent headed by the 'Lajkonik', a man dressed as a Tartar with a model horse attached to his waist. He advances slowly towards Rynek Główny, dancing to deafening music, imitating a rider's movements and hitting the spectators with his club to ensure their health and good fortune. His dance comes to an end at the *Sukiennice*, signalling the commencement of the *Dni Cracowa* (Cracow Days) festivities. When the Boatmen's Guild was disbanded the organisation of the festivities was entrusted to the Builders' Guild. The costume now used by the Lajkonik was designed in 1904 by Stanisław Wyspiański. It is probable that this guild pageant has its origins in ancient Slav rituals linked to Sun worship.

The Kościuszko mound - an earth mound built by the Polish people in memory of the hero of their own country and of the United States of America.

THE KOŚCIUSZKO MOUND

On a green hill above the city to the west of Zwierzyniec stands an unusual earth mound covered in grass and surrounded by a circle of brick buildings. The Kościuszko Mound, was built between 1821 and 1823 in memory of Tadeusz Kościuszko, a patriot and hero of the battle of Saratoga Springs. Leader of the 1794 uprising, he was defeated and seriously wounded in the last battle and was taken prisoner by the Russians and deported to St Petersburg. After two years he was freed by the Czar and allowed to live in exile in Switzerland. He died in 1817 away from his homeland. The mound in his honour was begun by Poles from all over the country bringing handfuls of soil and laying them in his memory. It stands thirty-four metres high and is surmounted by a boulder, brought from the Tatra mountains, inscribed with his name. The mound contains soil from the battlefields of Poland and America. At the time of the Austrian occu-pation of Cracow it was surrounded by fortifications, finished in 1853, which proved to be one of the city's major defences. The pyramidal form of the mound to Tadeusz Kościuszko is in keeping with ancient custom in Cracow. To the east of the city are two other myste-rious tumuli dateable to the 6th or 7th century. The Krak Tumulus and the Wanda Tumulus are allegedly the tombs of the founder of Cracow and of his daugh-ter. Archaeological research, however, has not provid-ed any evidence to support the funerary nature of the mounds. More probable is the theory linking these me-dieval mounds to astronomical studies: on 21 June from the Krak Tumulus the sun-rise is clearly visible on the Wanda Tumulus and on the winter solstice from the Wanda Tumulus the sun sets on the Krak Tumulus. The Kościuszko mound rises 326 metres above sea-level and affords an excellent panorama of the city and beyond; on a clear day one can see the Tatra mountains, some 100 kms from Cracow. In the 1930s a mound was raised in memory of Piłsudski on a nearby hill.

Two views of the Bielany Monastery on the
Silver Mountain - a Camaldolese hermitage.

BIELANY

The impressive Camaldolese monastery at Bielany is
perfectly visible from certain areas in Cracow. The
hermitage of the contemplative monastic community
was built far from the bustle and confusion of the city,
away from any major roads. The white church towers
against the greens of the surrounding woods create a
sense of peaceful harmony of architecture and nature.
The monastery is built on a hill known as 'the Silver
Mountain' overlooking Bielany village. Its situation
far from the centre of Cracow creates problems for visitors but is obviously more suited to the monks' life of
prayer and contemplation. Only male visitors can at-
tend Sunday morning Mass, and females can only at-
tend the rare Masses celebrated for the general public.
The monastery was built in the first half of the 17th
century by Andrea Spezzo and Giovanni Seccatori and
was founded by Mikołaj Wolski, the King's marshall,
who at the beginning of the 17th century brought the
Camaldolese monks from Italy, promising them the
choice of site on which to build their monastery. The
monks chose this spot, on land not belonging to the
marshal but to Prince Sebastian Lubomirski. Wolski
therefore invited his neighbour the Prince to a splendid
dinner and having explained his difficulty was given
the land as a gesture of friendship. Much moved by the
generosity of the Prince, Wolski then packed all the
silver used at the dinner into boxes and sent it to
Lubomirski. From that day the hill became known as
the Silver Mountain. The baroque interior of the
Bielany church is famous for its 17th-century paintings, especially those by Tommaso Dolabella, a
Venetian who became the most celebrated painter in
Poland in the first half of the 17th century, working for
three kings of the Vasa dynasty. He is best known for
his epic works drawing on Polish stylistic tradition,
and he had many followers.

View of Tyniec Abbey - Wawel might once have had
a similar appearance.

TYNIEC

Reflected in the still waters of the Vistula we can see
white rocks, surmounted by an old wall surrounding
the Benedictine abbey of Tyniec, one of the oldest
monasteries in Poland. The date of the monks' arrival
on the limestone hill is not known but in both its formation and shape it is reminiscent of Wawel. We do
know that they settled at Tyniec either during the reign
of Casimir the Restorer (1038-54) or of his successor

Boleslaw the Bold (1054-79). By the end of the 11th
century the monastery was already active and the
Benedictines were engaged in the painstaking work of
copying books and manuscripts. The name *Tyniec* de-
rived from the old word *tyn* meaning enclosure or
wall, gives us some indication of the ancient history of
settlements on this hill. The legend about a certain
Walgierz Udały, recorded in medieval chronicles, suggests that as early as the pagan era the manor on the
hill belonged to a powerful feudal lord. The architec-

tural history on the limestone hill begins with the foundation of the abbey. The first romanesque church was on a basilican plan with a triple apse. In the 15th century it was altered in the gothic style, while in the first half of the 17th century it was decorated according to baroque taste. For many centuries the Tyniec Abbey was the major centre for theological studies in Poland and enjoyed considerable economic power. The monastery owned some hundred villages and a few cities. In 1817 it was suppressed and the buildings remained empty until 1939, when the monks returned. In the 1960s as part of the celebrations to mark the millennium of Poland's conversion to Christianity (966-1966) the monastery sponsored the translation of the Bible into Polish. The "Millennium Bible" proved to be an excellent translation both because of the beauty of its language and for its great theological interest. The abbey church is a basilica with a central nave and single side aisles, with the façade flanked by two massive towers. The splendid baroque interior includes an 18th-

Aerial views of Tyniec Abbey, an
11th-century Benedictine Abbey.

century altar in black marble (a favourite material at
this time) designed by Francesco Placidi (1710-82), an
Italian architect who had worked in Dresden before
being summoned to Poland by King Augustus III of
Saxony in 1742. The present monastery buildings date
from the 15th to the 17th century but some fragments
of the original romanesque structure survive. They suffered considerable damage when they were abandoned
in the 19th century, but were restored when the monks
returned in 1939. There is an exhibition on the history
of the monastery open to visitors in the rooms next to
the church. In the 1950s and 1960s extensive archaeological excavations were carried out on the hill and the
finds were described as "sensational". These included
the tombs of the abbots who lived in the 11th and 12th
century containing precious objects, so that one became
known as the "tomb of the golden abbot" and the other
"the tomb of the silver abbot". Among the pieces discovered were a gold romanesque chalice and paten and
a golden pastoral staff, now displayed in the Wawel
Cathedral Treasury. There is an interesting 18th-centu-
ry well in the abbey courtyard which is so deep that its
water level is the same as the Vistula which runs far
below at the foot of the hill. The monastery of Tyniec,
although some ten kilometres outside Cracow, has always been closely linked to the history of the capital,
while the village of Tyniec only became part of Cracow
in 1973. It is in this village in the *Pod Lutym Turem* inn
that the first chapters of Henryk Sienkiewicz's novel
Krzyzacy (The Teutonic Knights) is set.

Pieskowa Skała Castle, near Cracow.

PIESKOWA SKAŁA

The Vistula, flowing through Cracow from west to east, divides the Carpathian foothills, to the south of the city, from the Jurassic limestone cliffs of Cracow-Częstochowa. Between 1333 and 1346 Casimir the Great built a chain of fortresses on the rocky peaks on the border with Silesia to defend Poland against attacks by John of Luxembourg. Known as "eagles' nests" these fortresses were so built as to enable each one to communicate with its two neighbours by means of flares. The fortress of Pieskowa Skała was positioned between Ojcow, which passed on communications to Wawel, and those castles further to the north. Some 25 km from Cracow, Pieskowa is often called the "Little Wawel", not so much because it houses part of the Wawel State Art Collections but for its renaissance courtyard modelled on the one at Wawel. The position of the Pieskowa Skała fortress was of the greatest strategic importance: it is built on a rocky peak with sheer drops from three sides of its walls. Even before Casimir the Great had the gothic castle built a wooden structure had stood on this point. From 1377 Pieskowa Skała became part of the property of the powerful Szafraniec family. Piotr Szafraniec received it as a gift from Louis d'Anjou in amends for the offence given him by one of the king's Hungarian soldiers. In 1542 Hieronim Szafraniec, secretary to King Sigismund I started to restore the castle, a labour which lasted, with intervals until 1580. The result of that restoration is the beautiful structure we see today, inspired by Italian renaissance models, considered the finest 16th-century magnate's castle to have survived in Poland. The castle houses two exhibitions: one devoted to the *History of the Pieskowa Skała Castle* and the other to *Stylistic changes in European Art from the Middle Ages to the first half of the Eighteenth Century.* The restaurant in one of the towers affords fine views of the terrace and the formal garden beyond the castle walls.

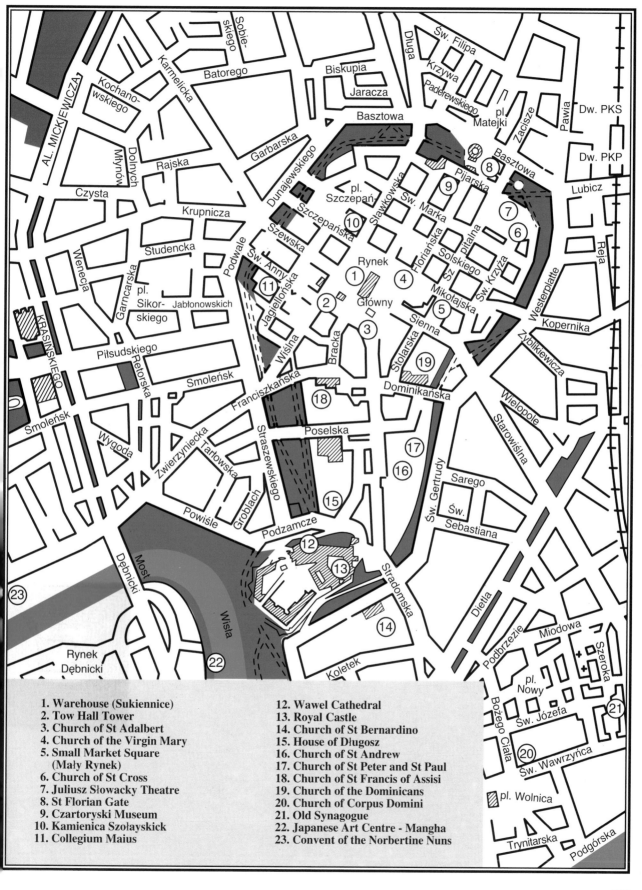

1. Warehouse (Sukiennice)
2. Tow Hall Tower
3. Church of St Adalbert
4. Church of the Virgin Mary
5. Small Market Square (Mały Rynek)
6. Church of St Cross
7. Juliusz Słowacky Theatre
8. St Florian Gate
9. Czartoryski Museum
10. Kamienica Szołayskick
11. Collegium Maius
12. Wawel Cathedral
13. Royal Castle
14. Church of St Bernardino
15. House of Długosz
16. Church of St Andrew
17. Church of St Peter and St Paul
18. Church of St Francis of Assisi
19. Church of the Dominicans
20. Church of Corpus Domini
21. Old Synagogue
22. Japanese Art Centre - Mangha
23. Convent of the Norbertine Nuns

INDEX